Welcome to the Magical World of Colors!

Get ready to embark on a colorful adventure filled with fairies, butterflies, and unicorns. Let your imagination soar as you bring these enchanting characters to life with your vibrant creativity. Have fun exploring and expressing yourself through the magic of coloring. Enjoy every moment of this magical journey

Everton Oliveira Monteiro

2024

This Book Belongs to:

○―――――――――――――――――○

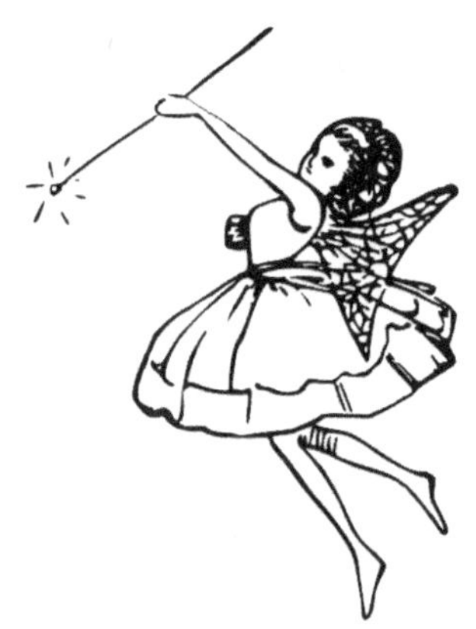

Test Color Page

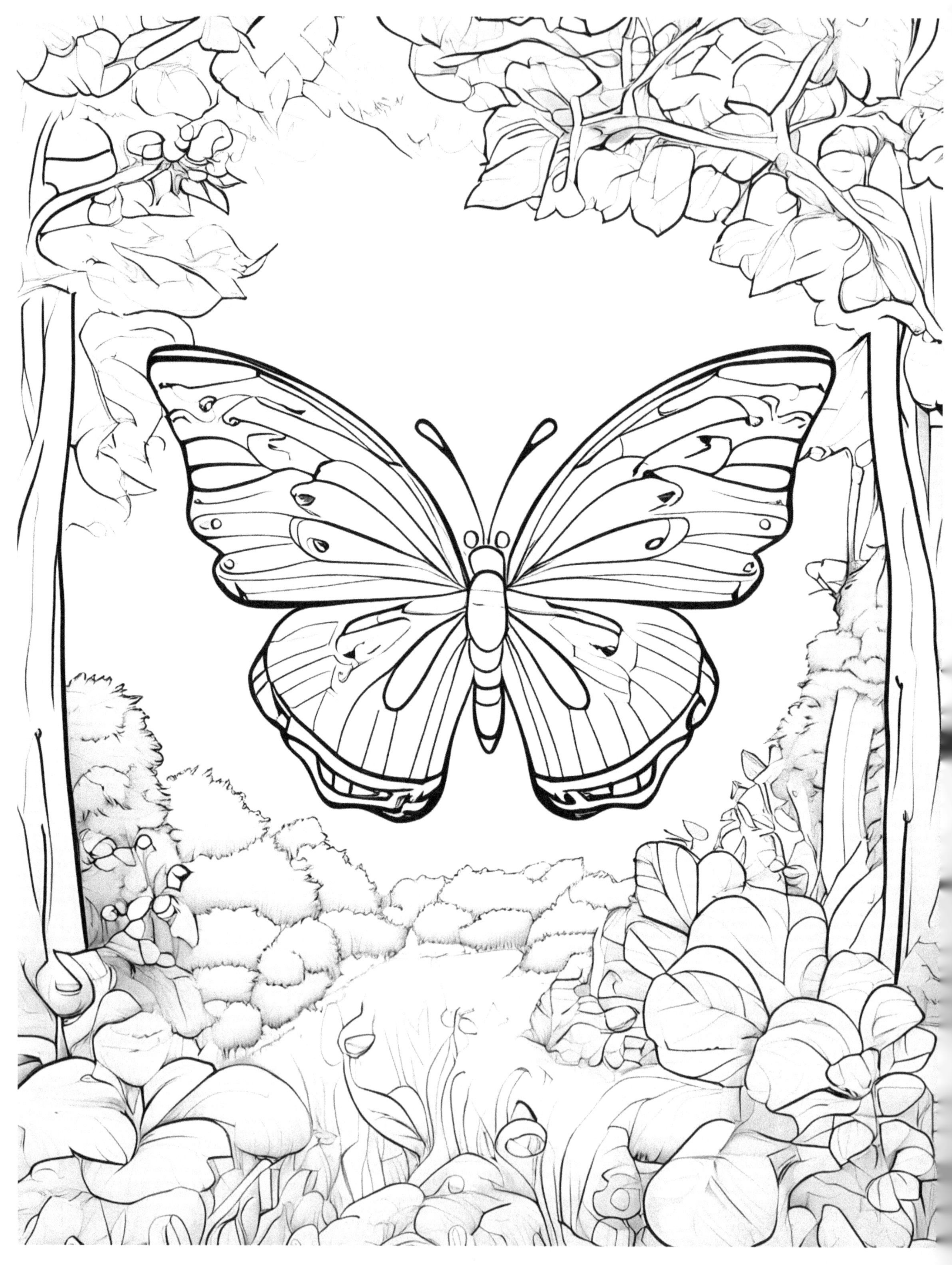

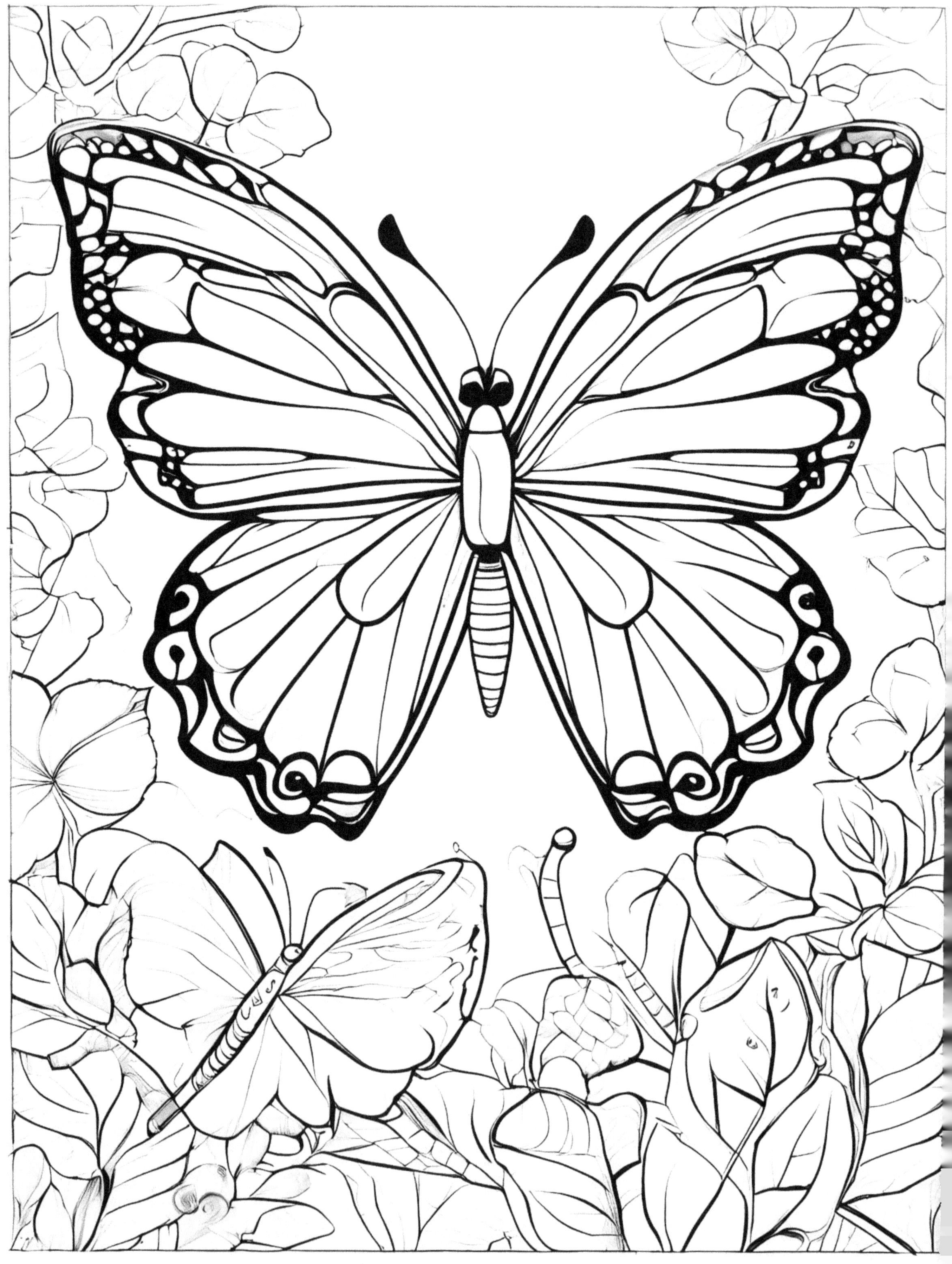

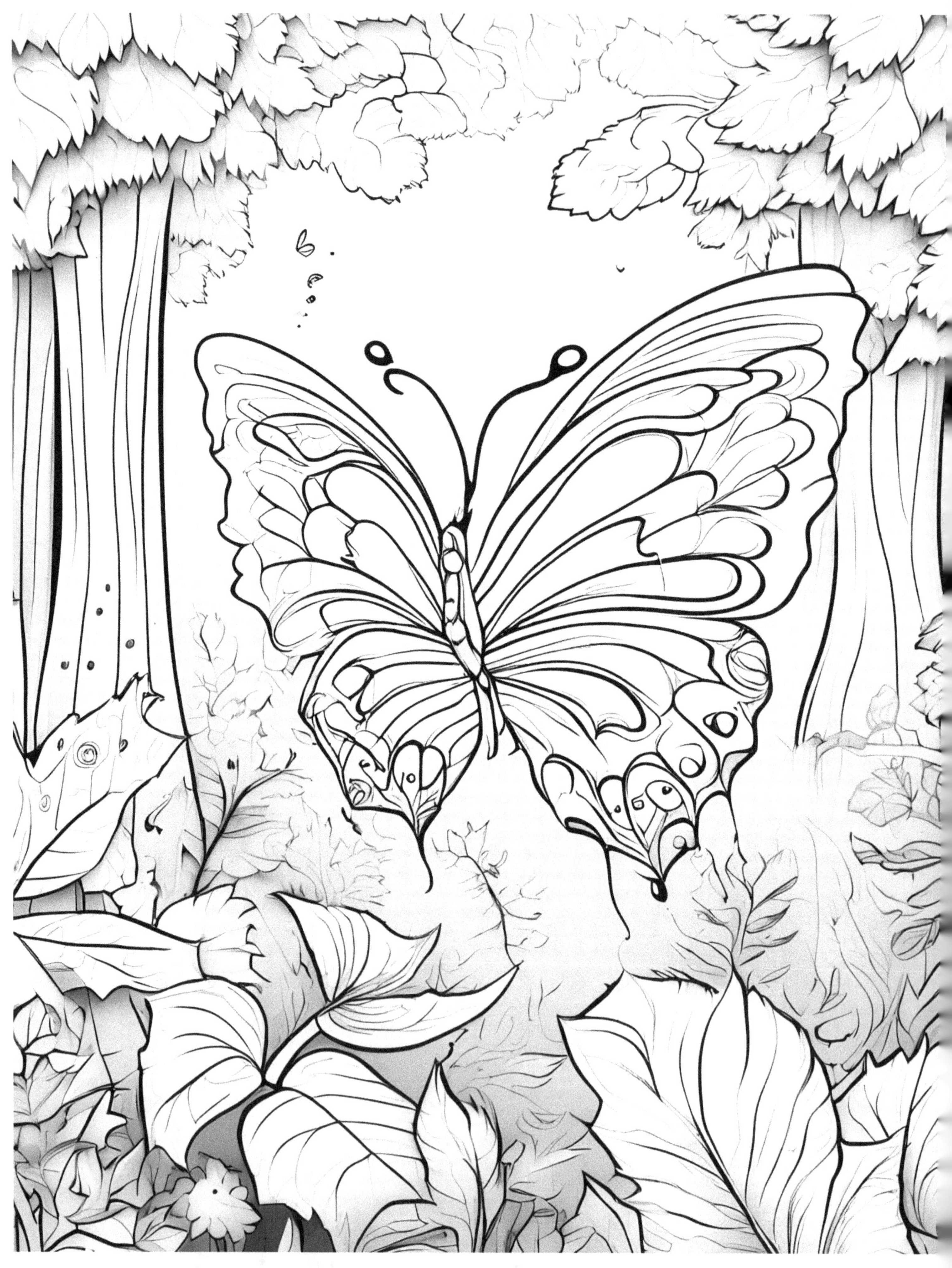

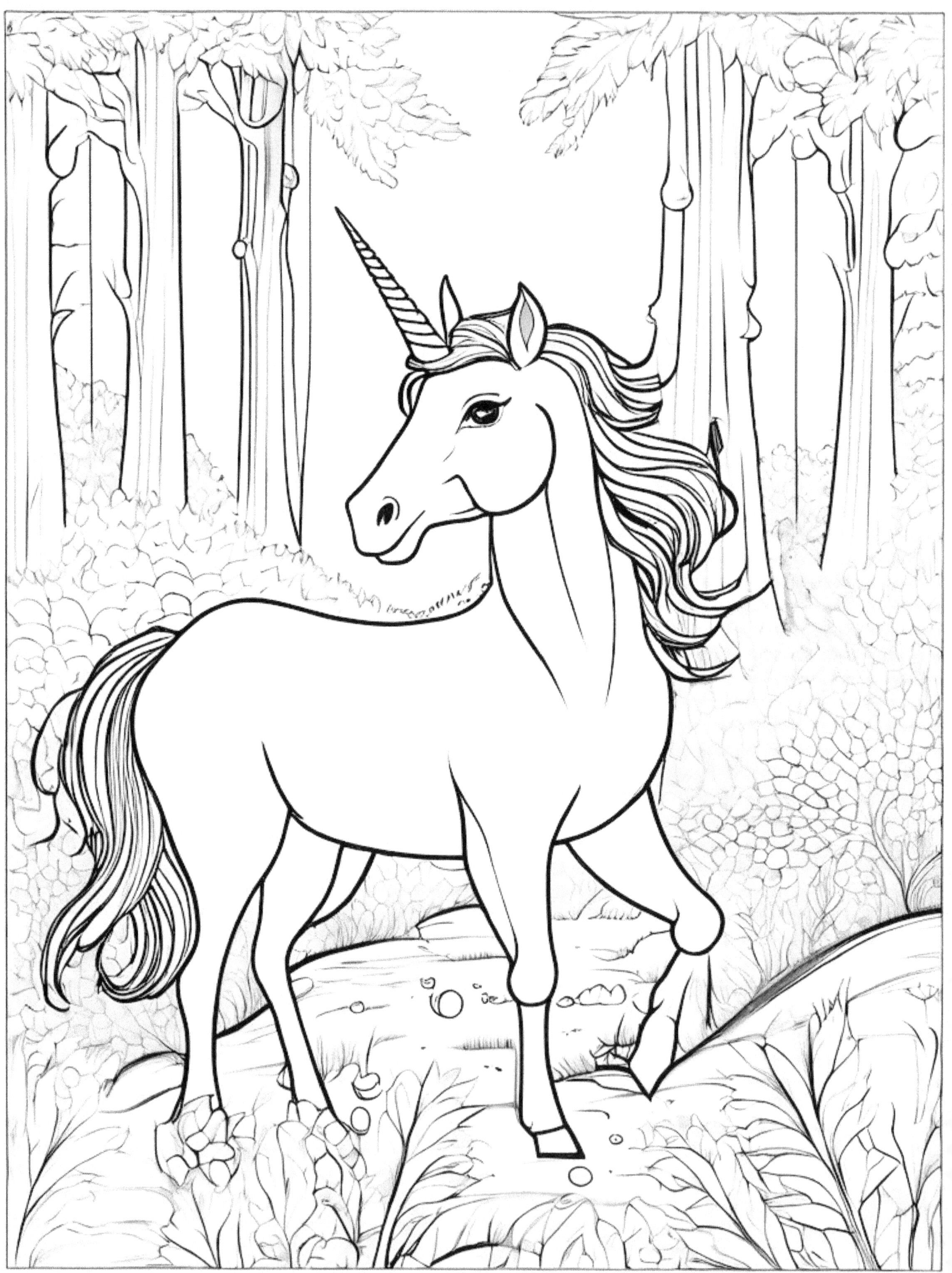

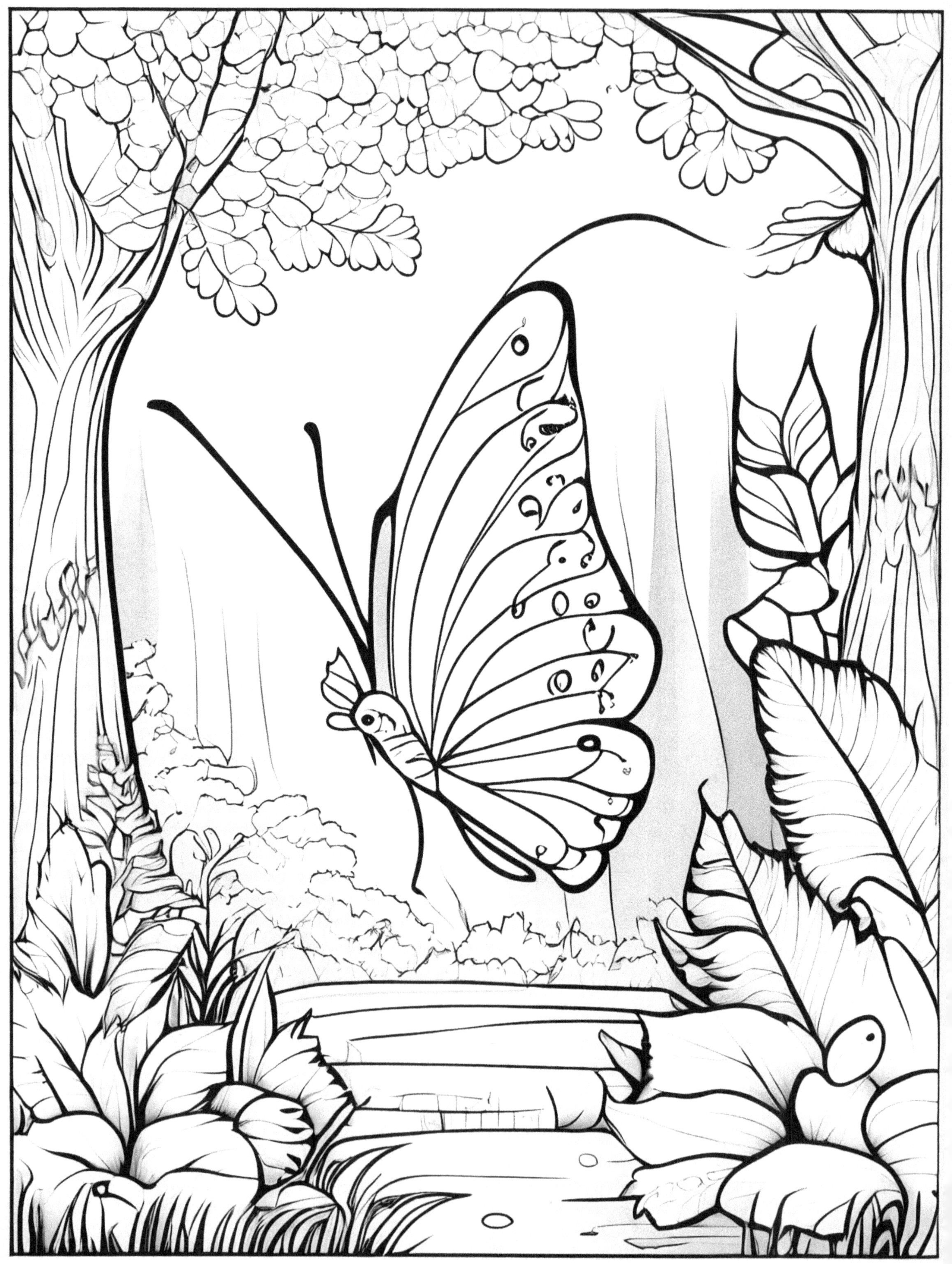

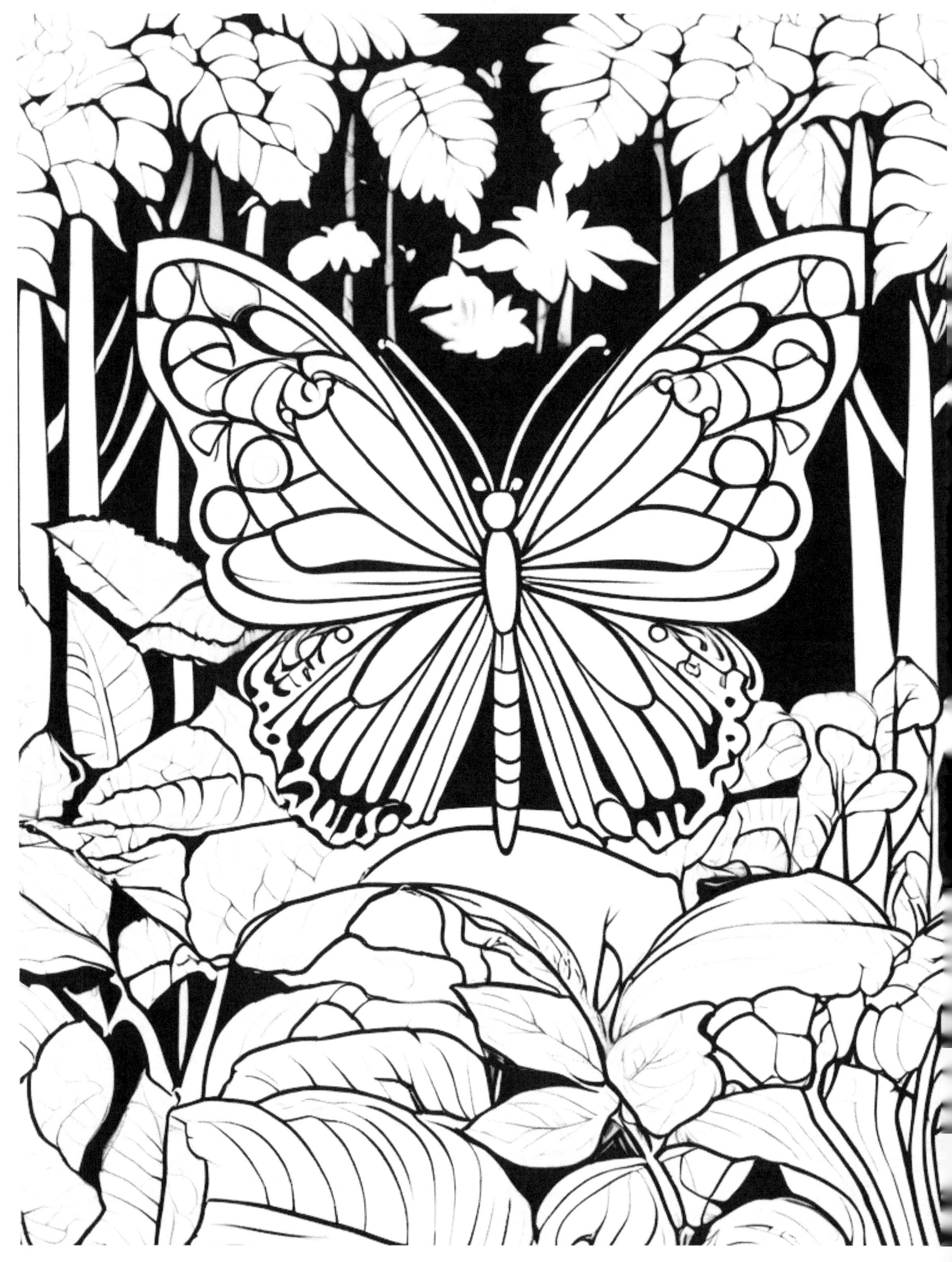

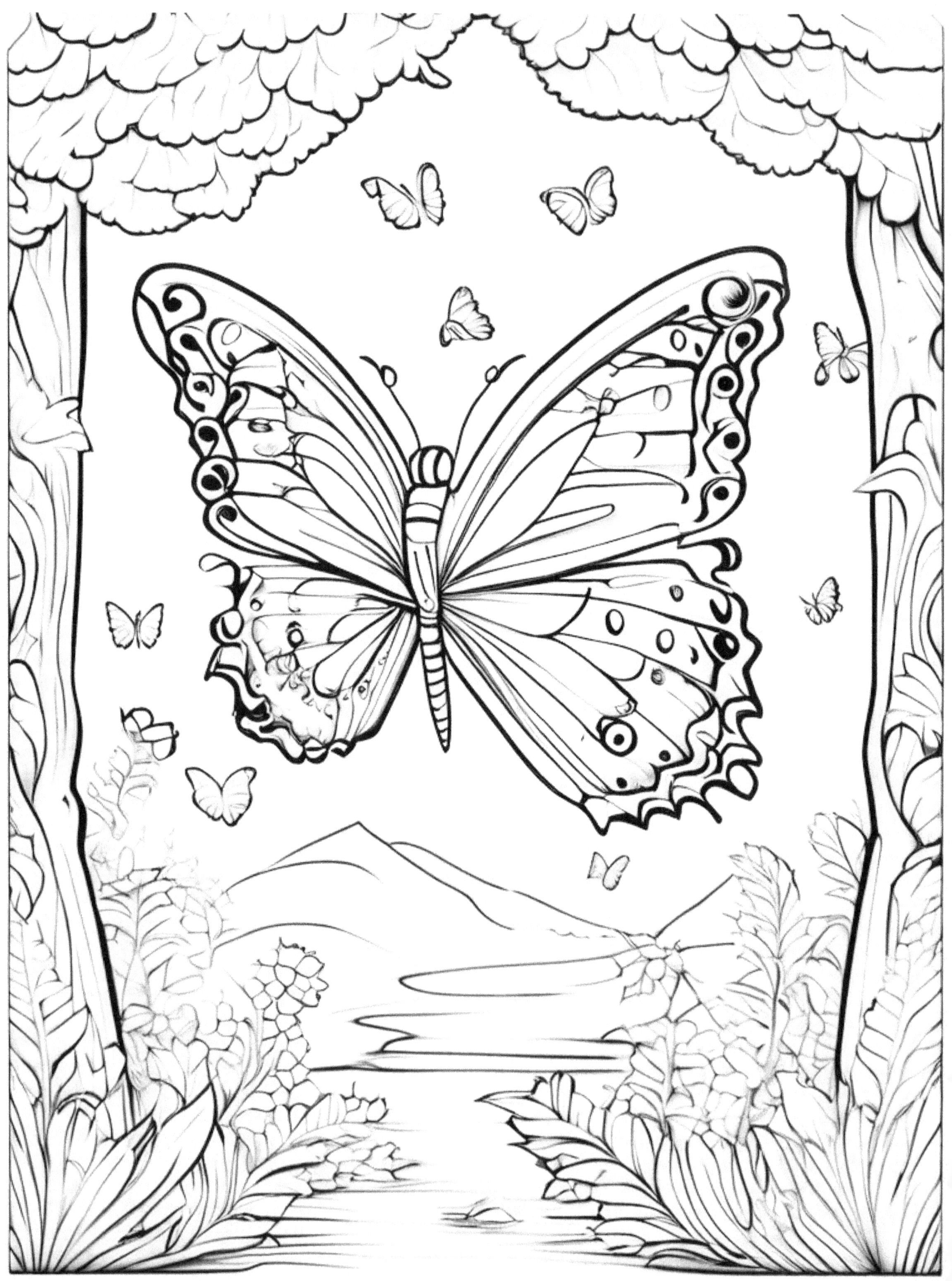

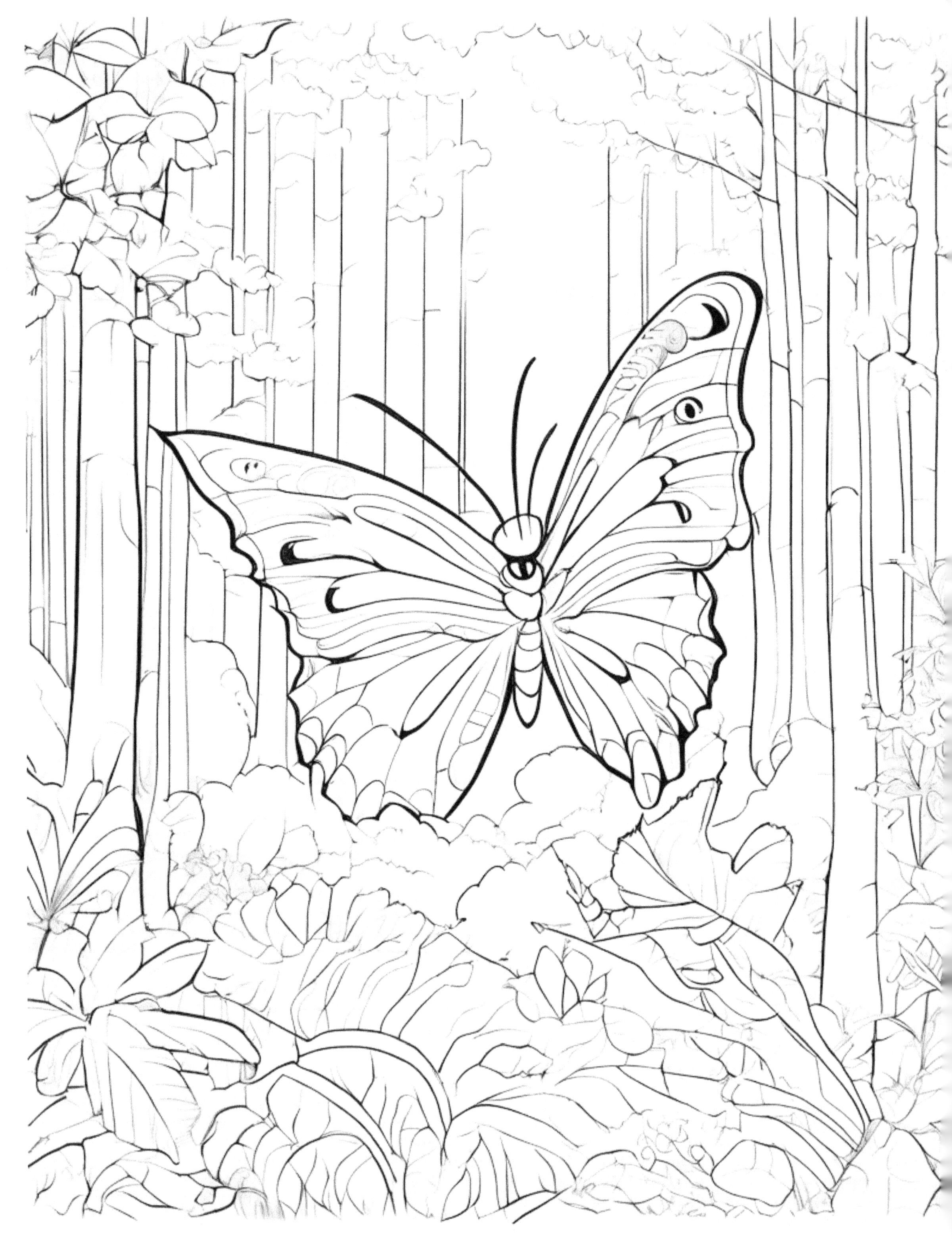

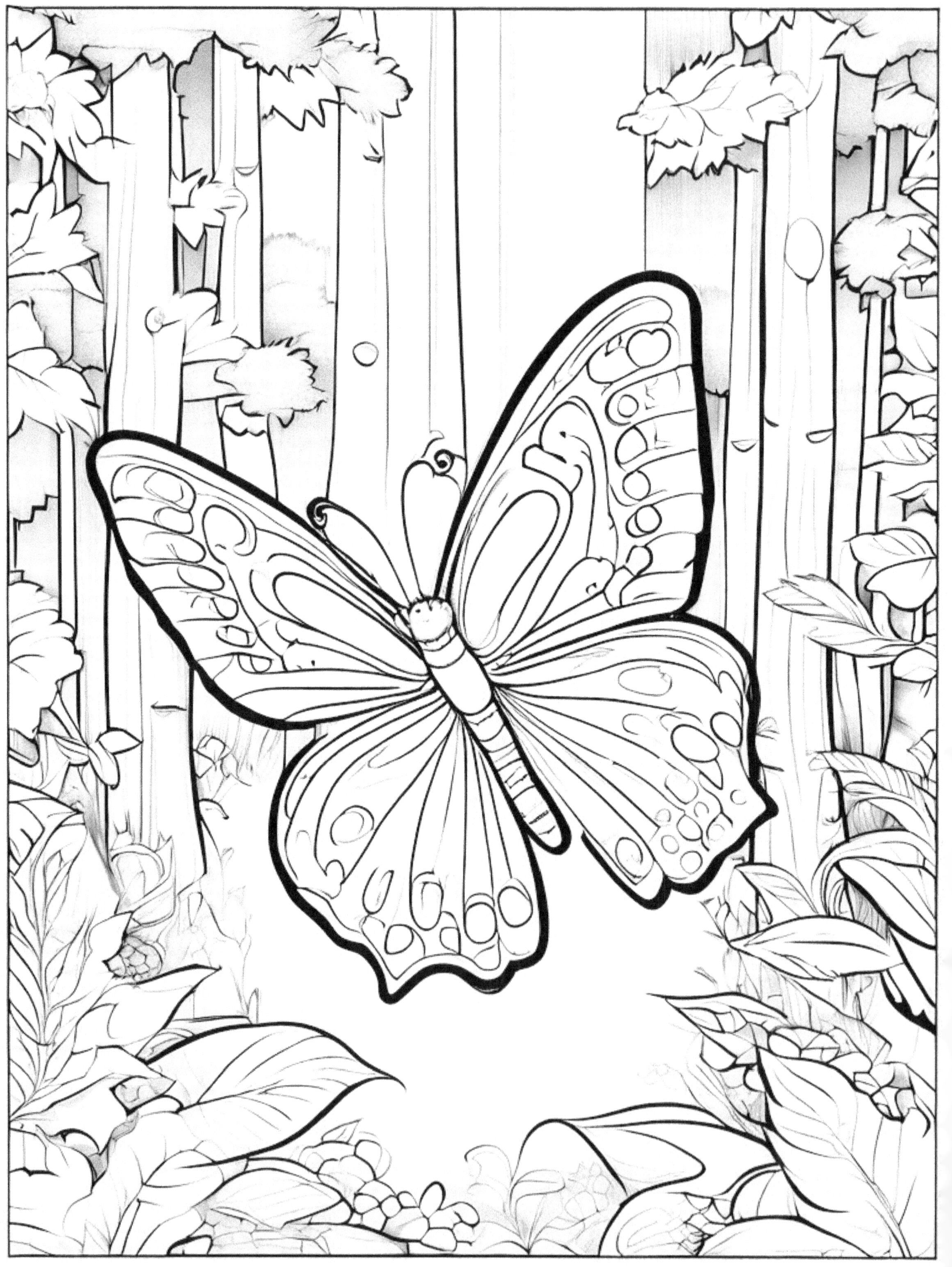

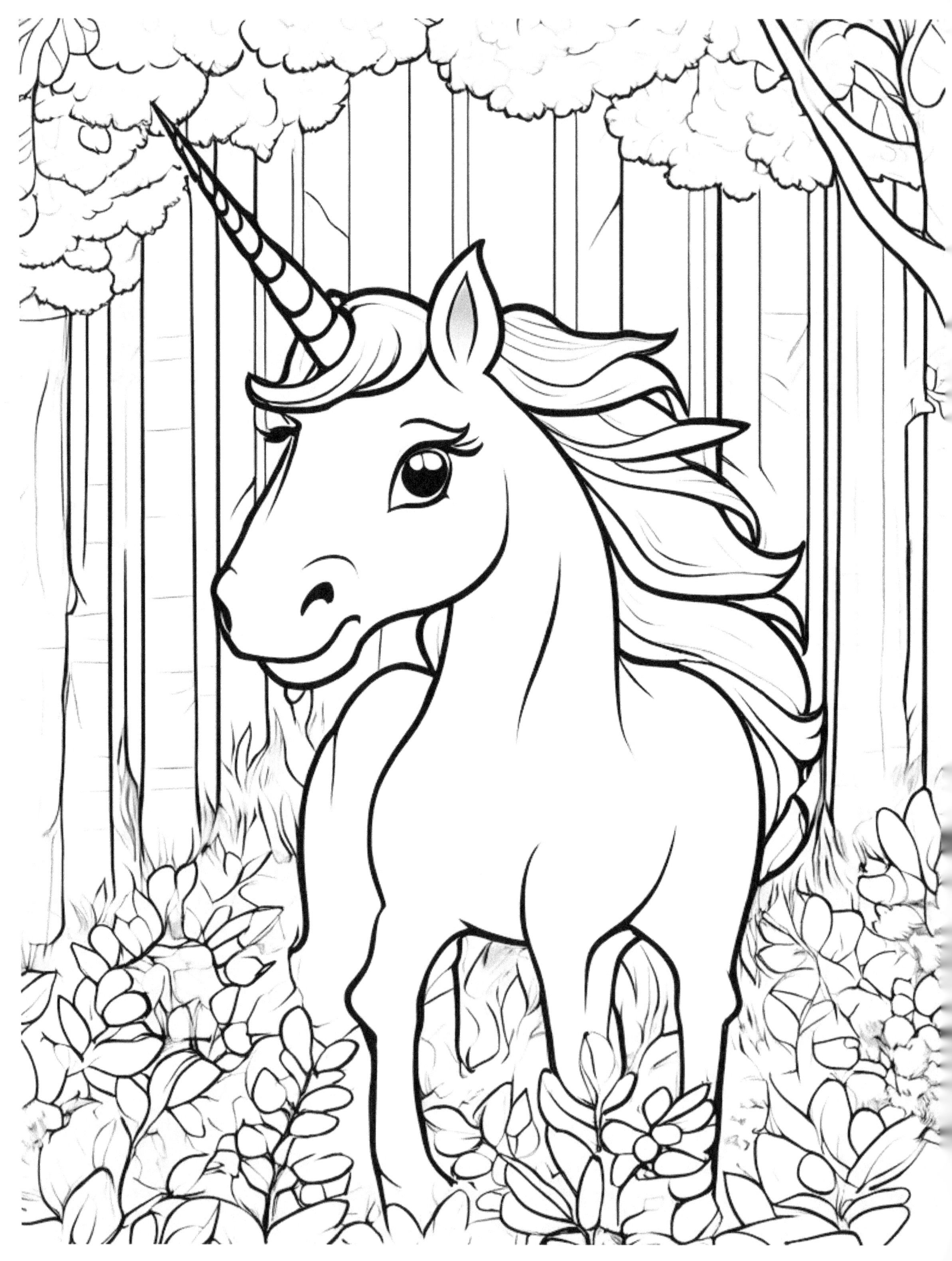

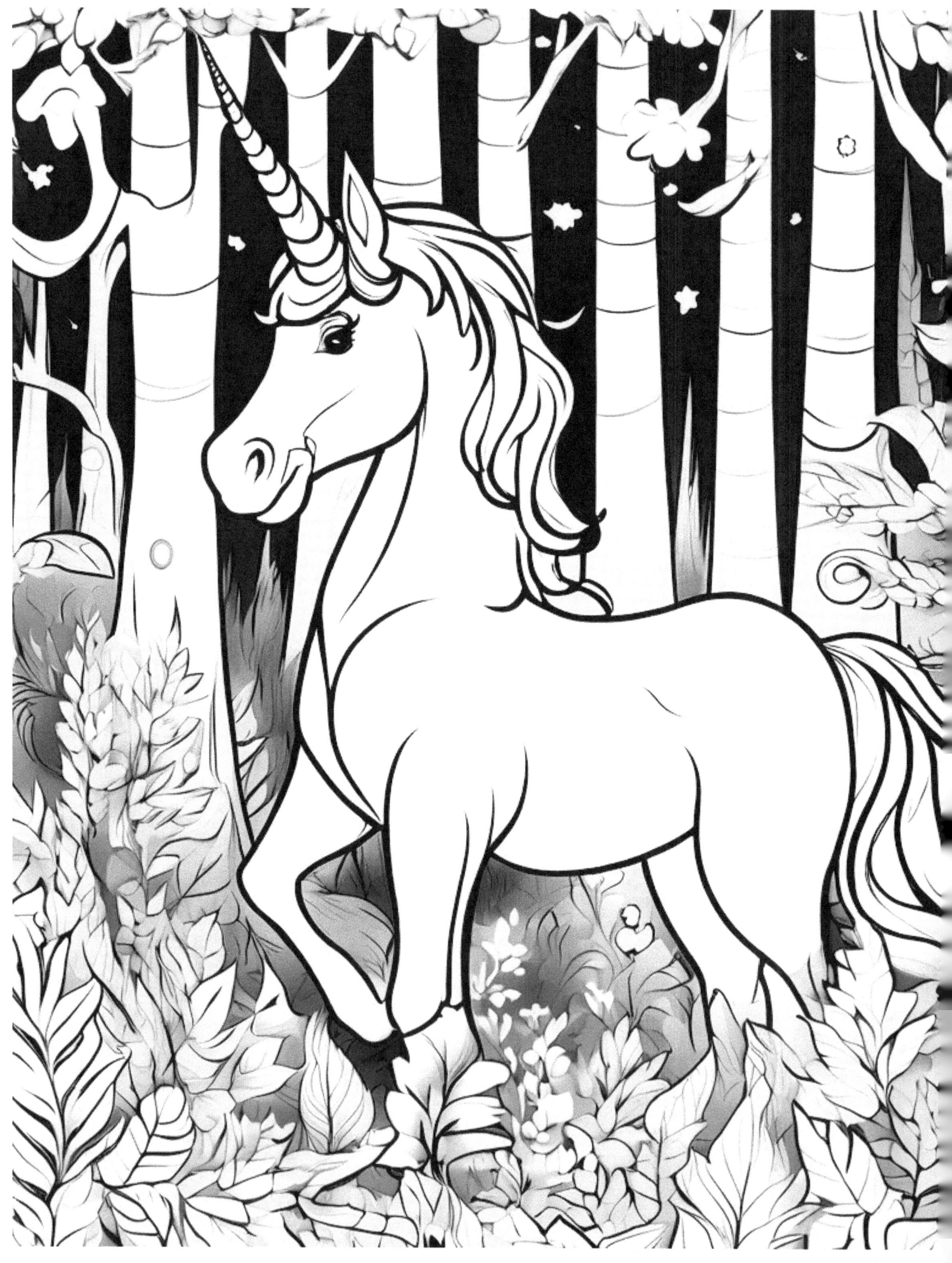

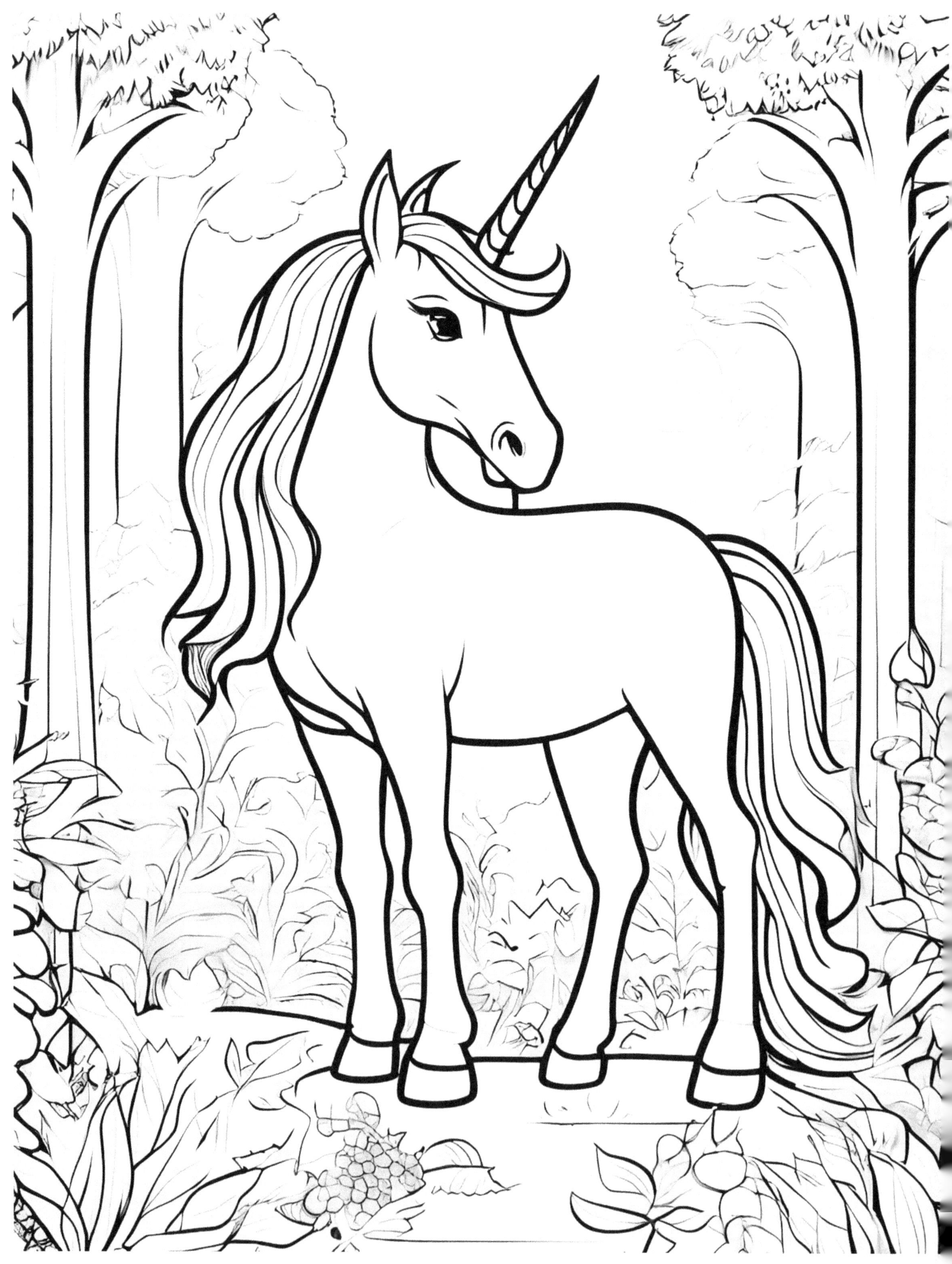

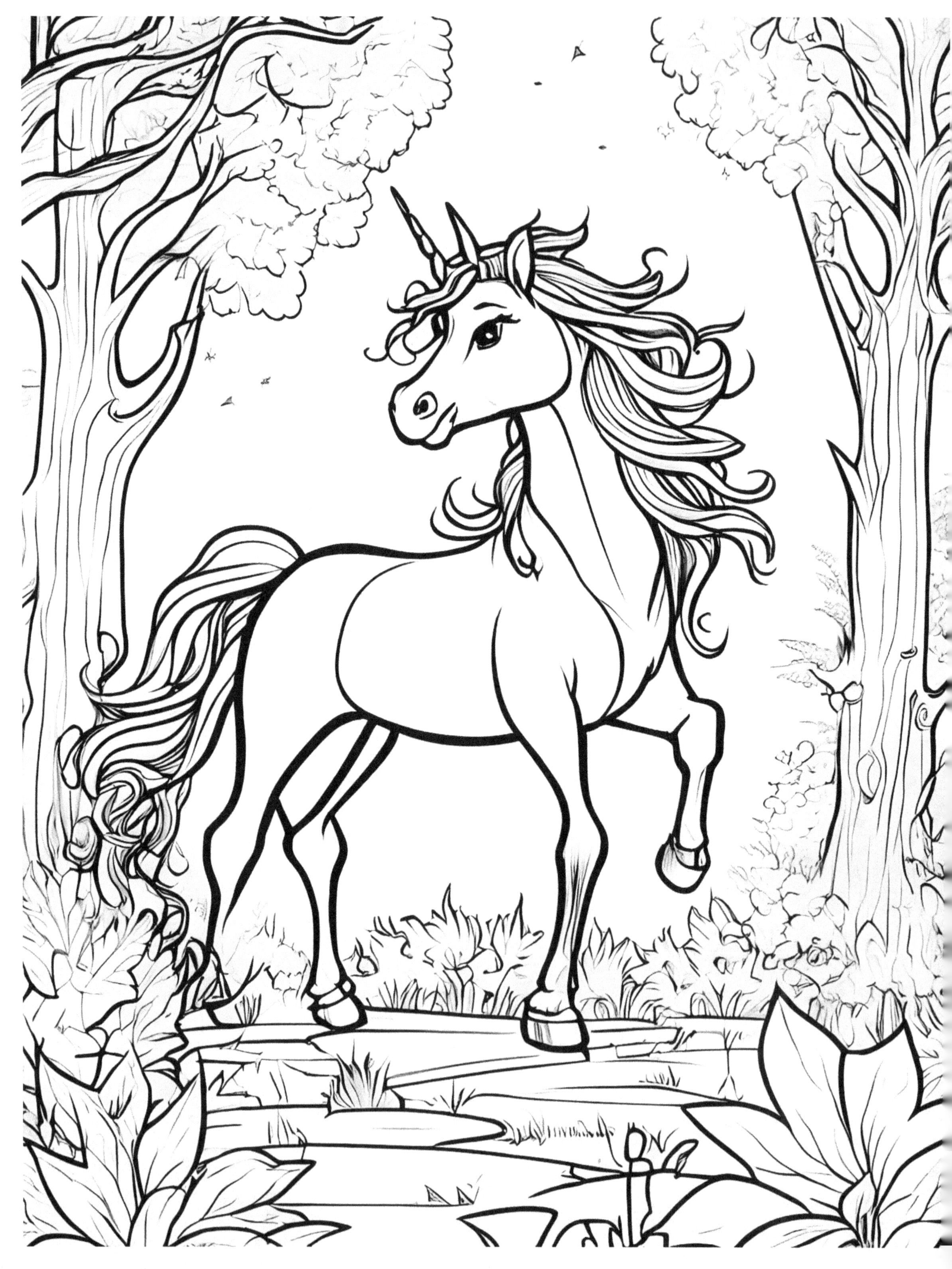

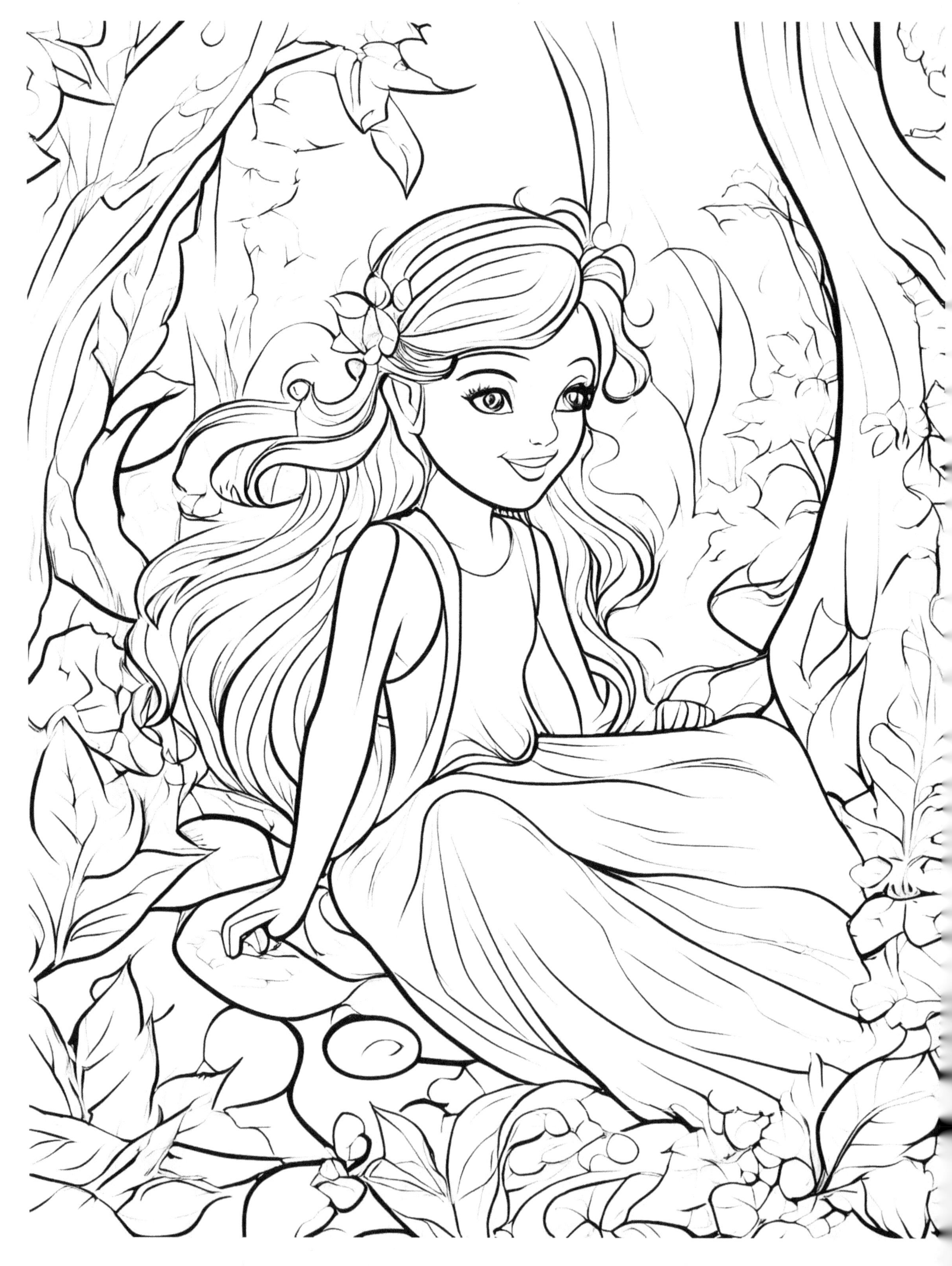

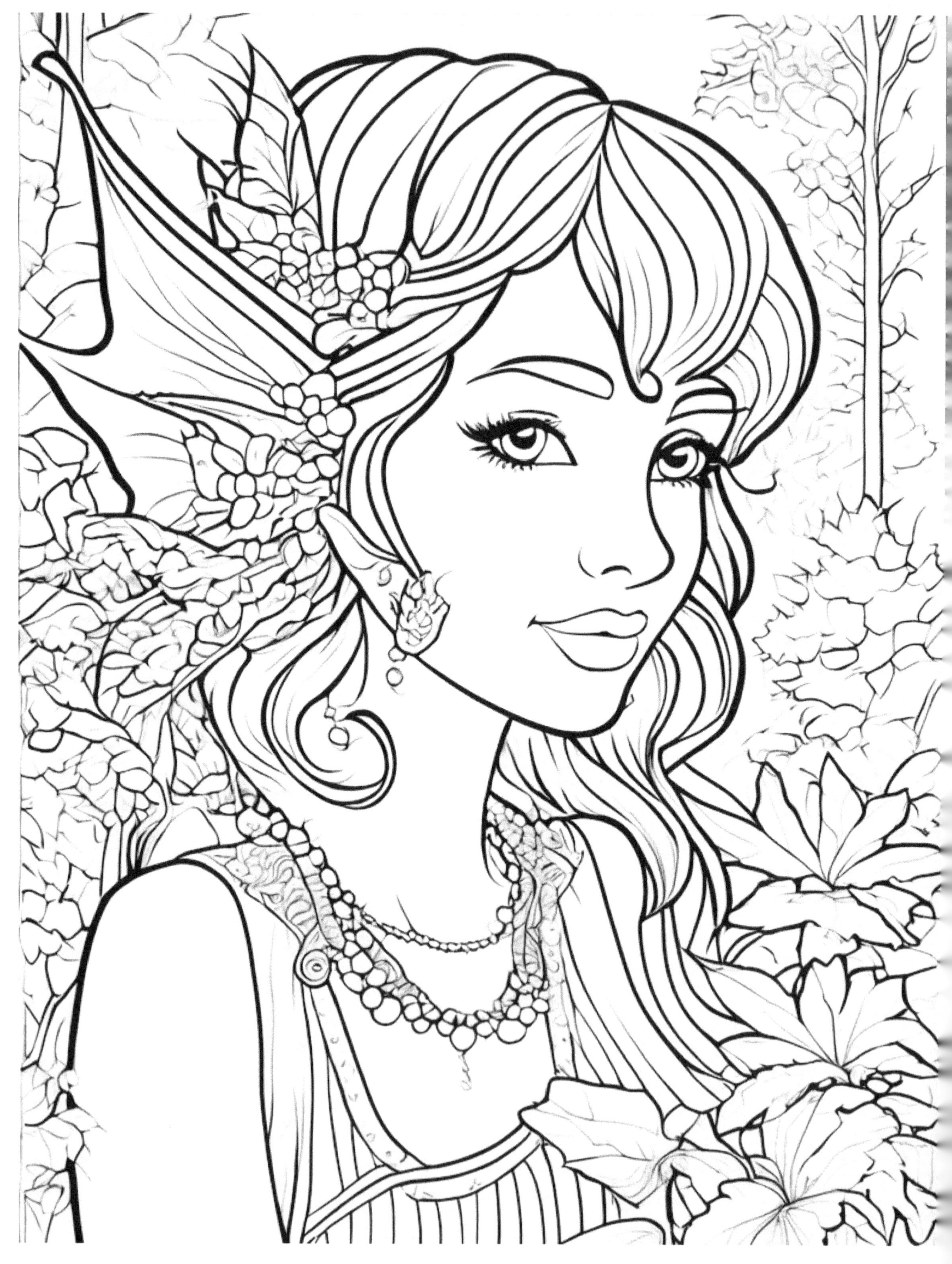

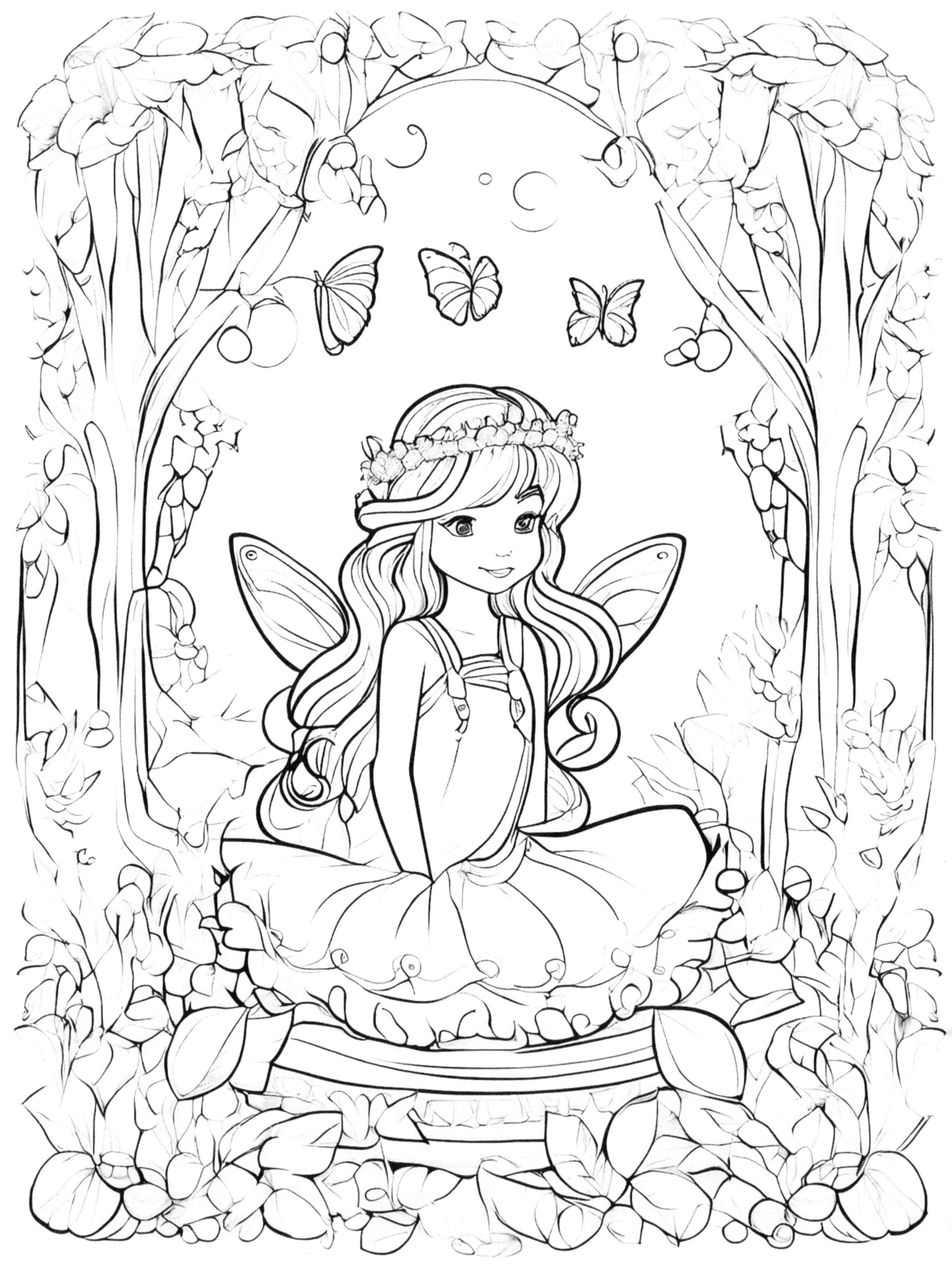

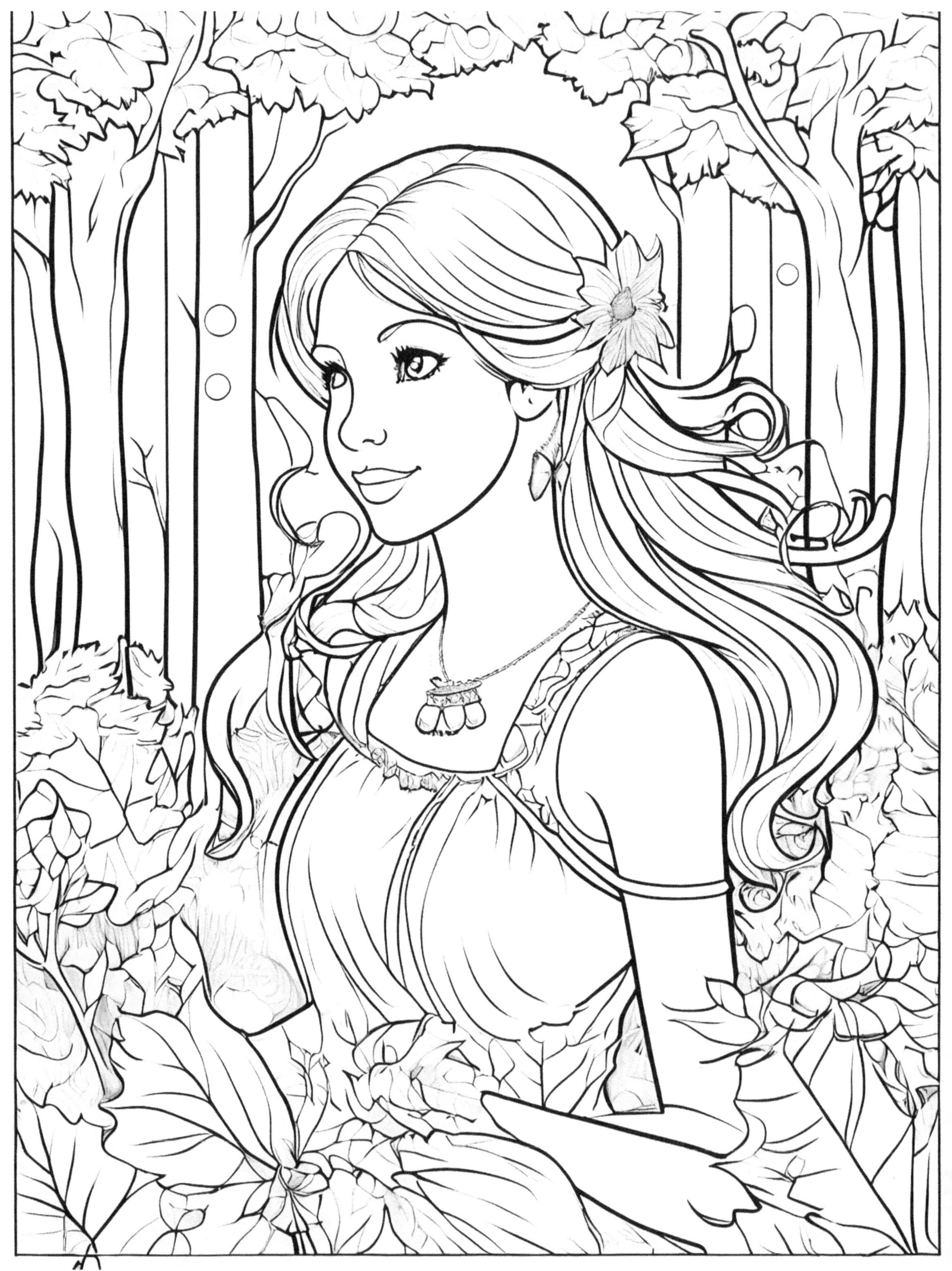

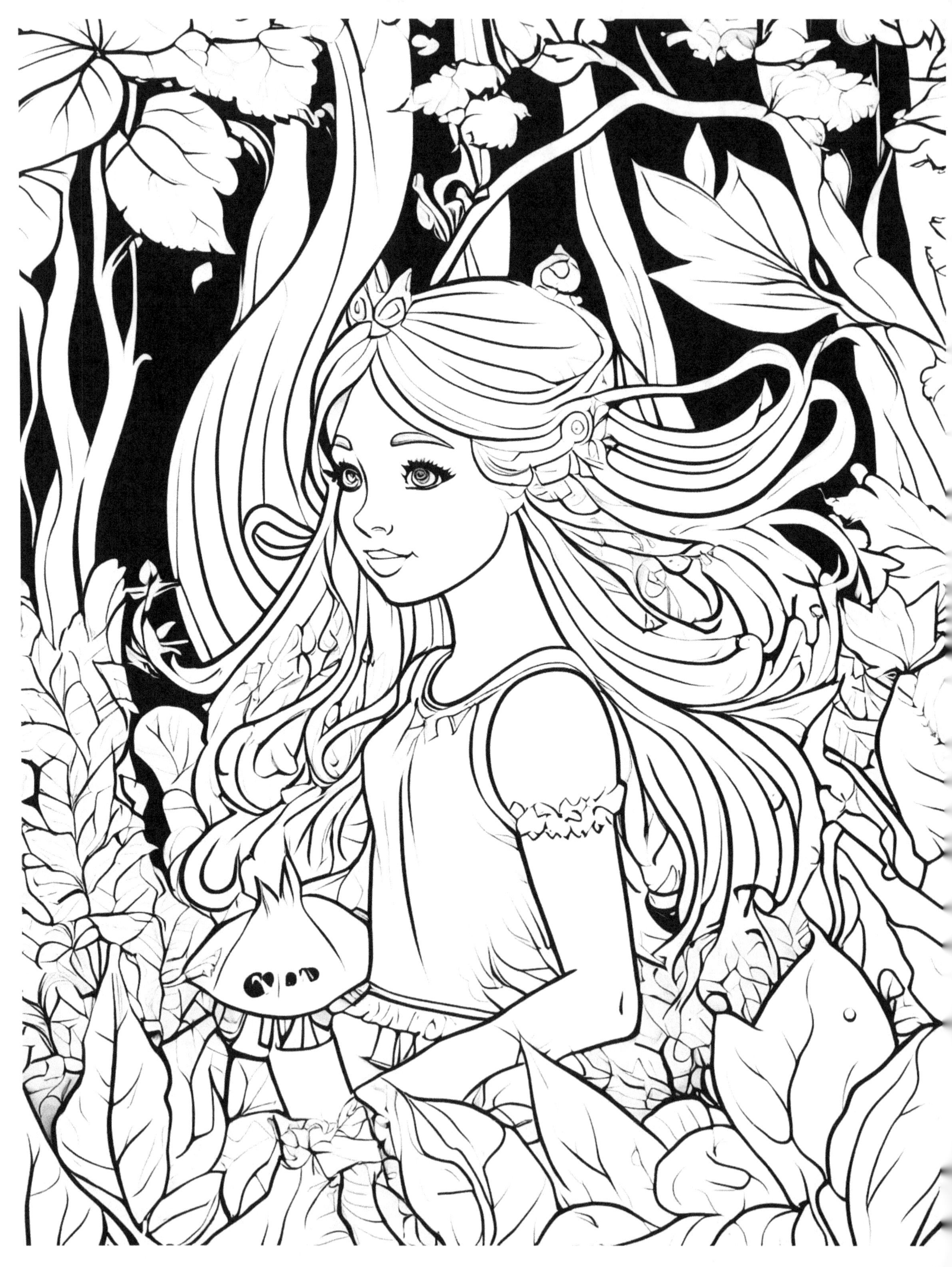

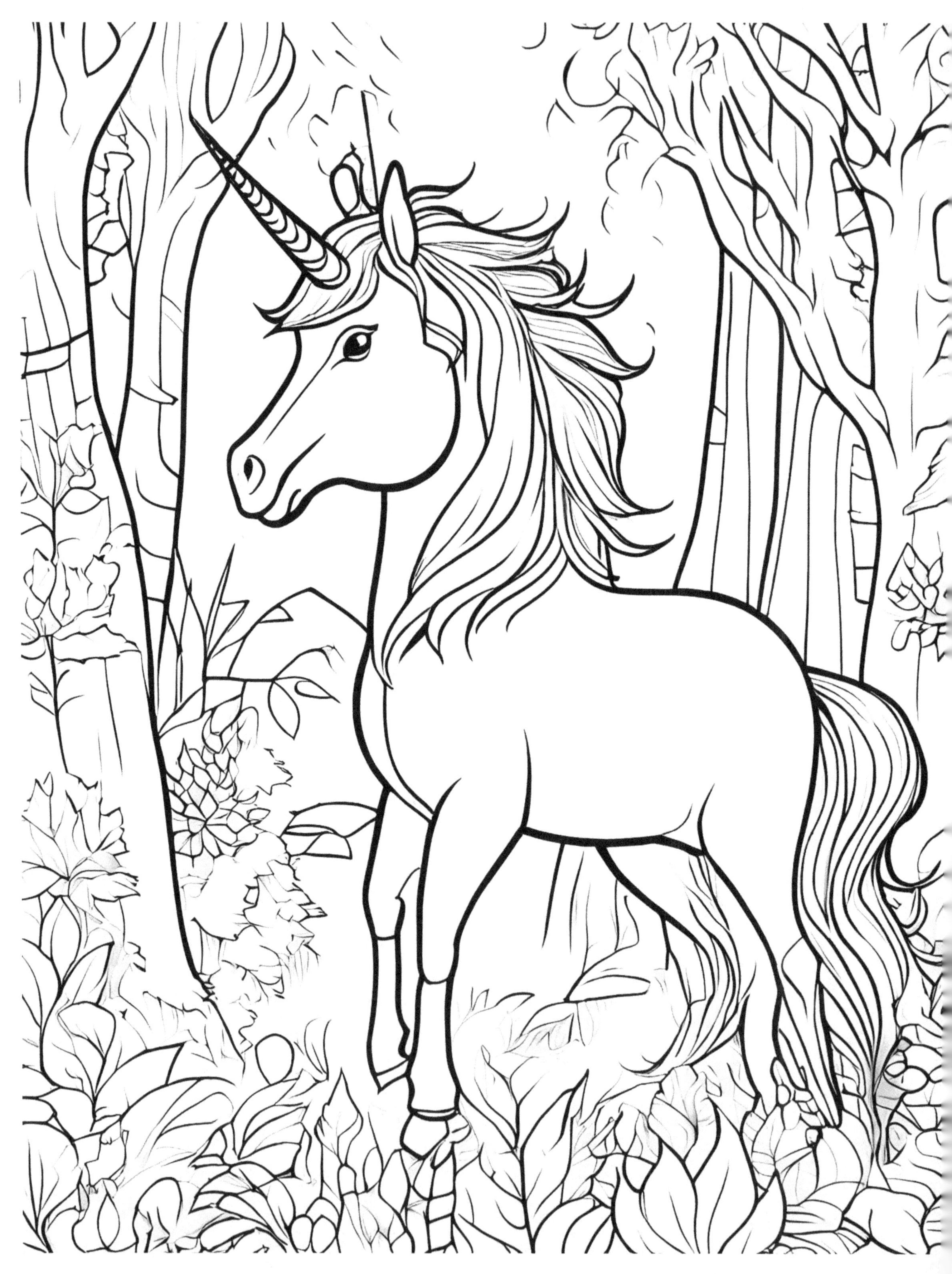

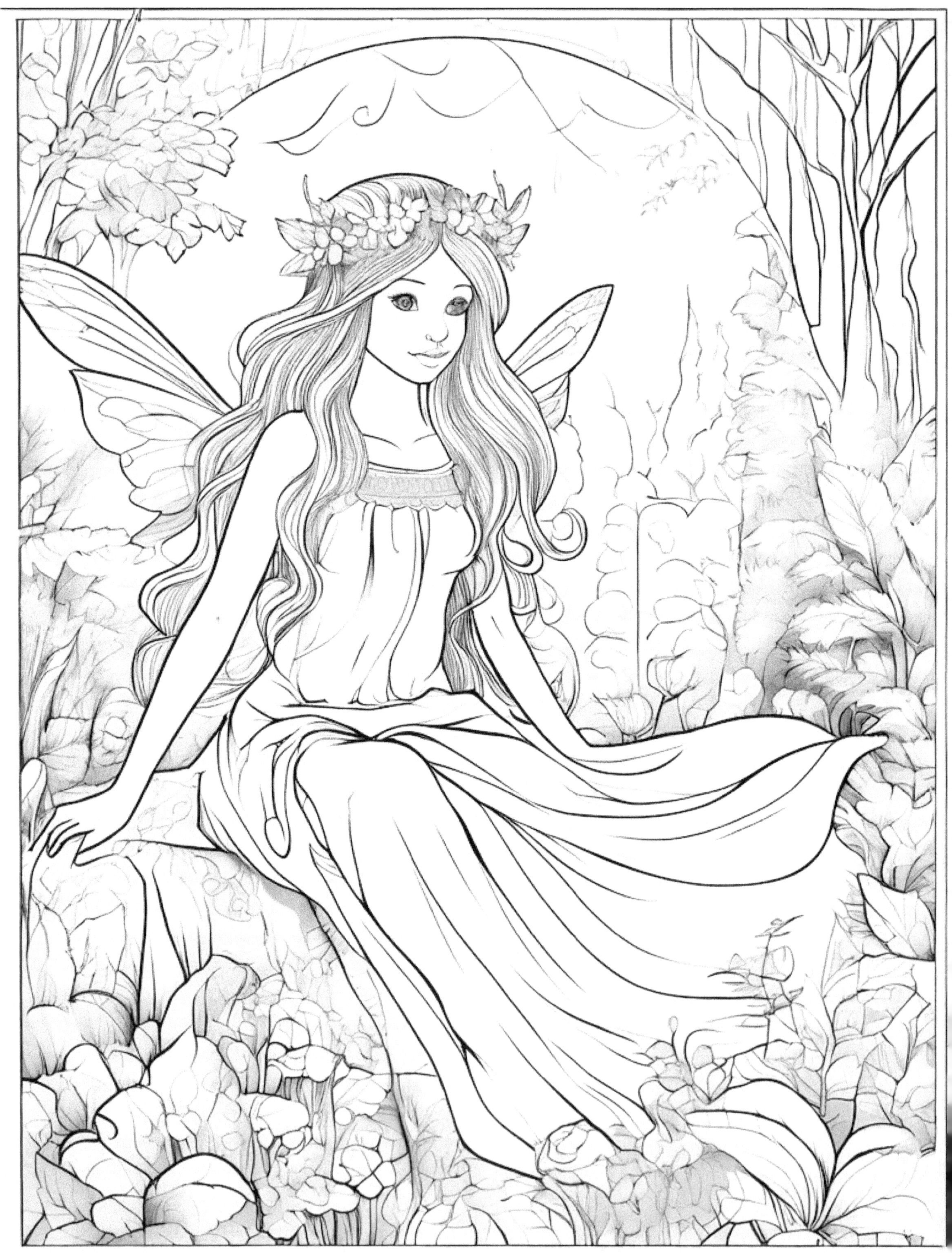

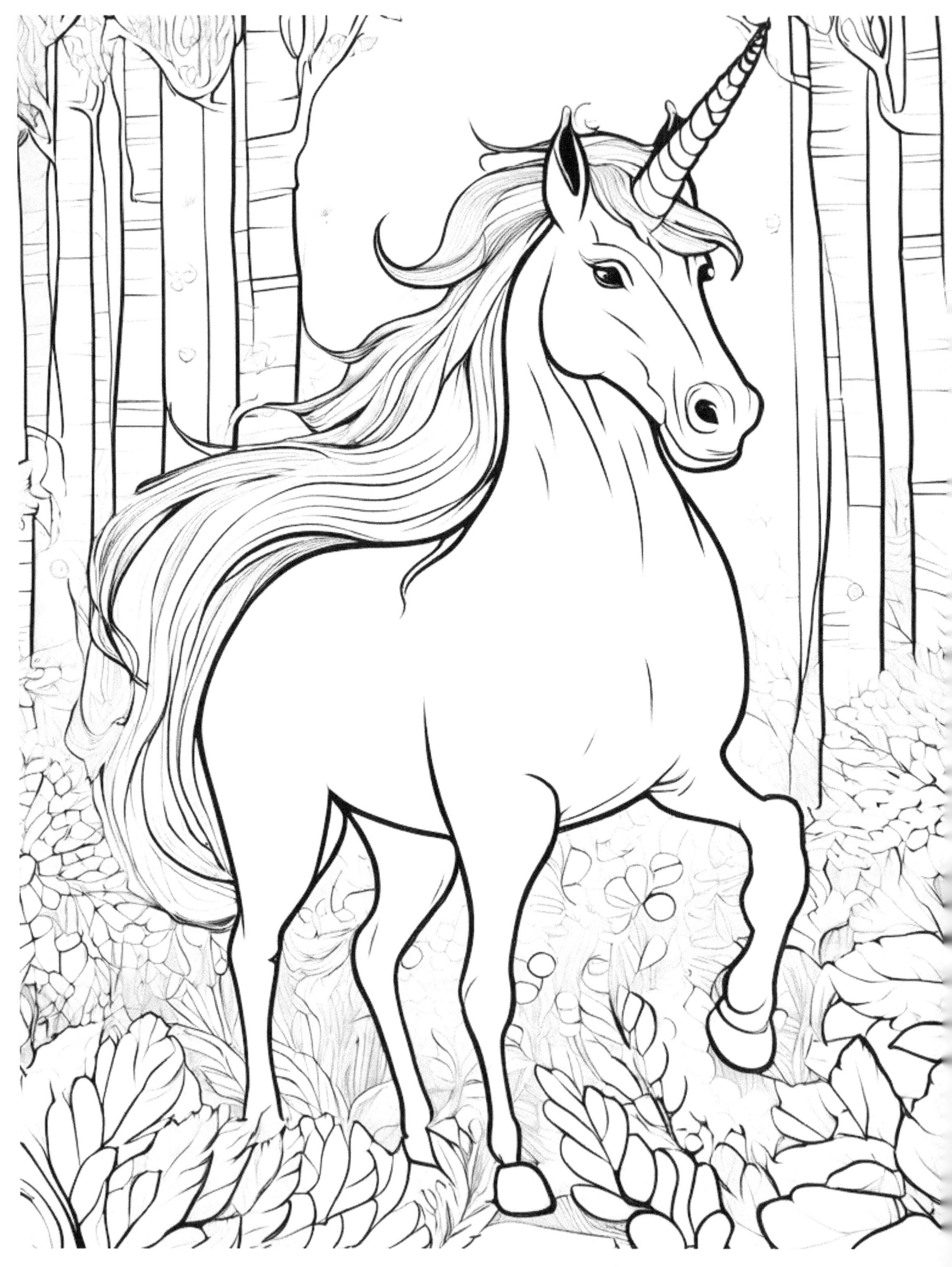

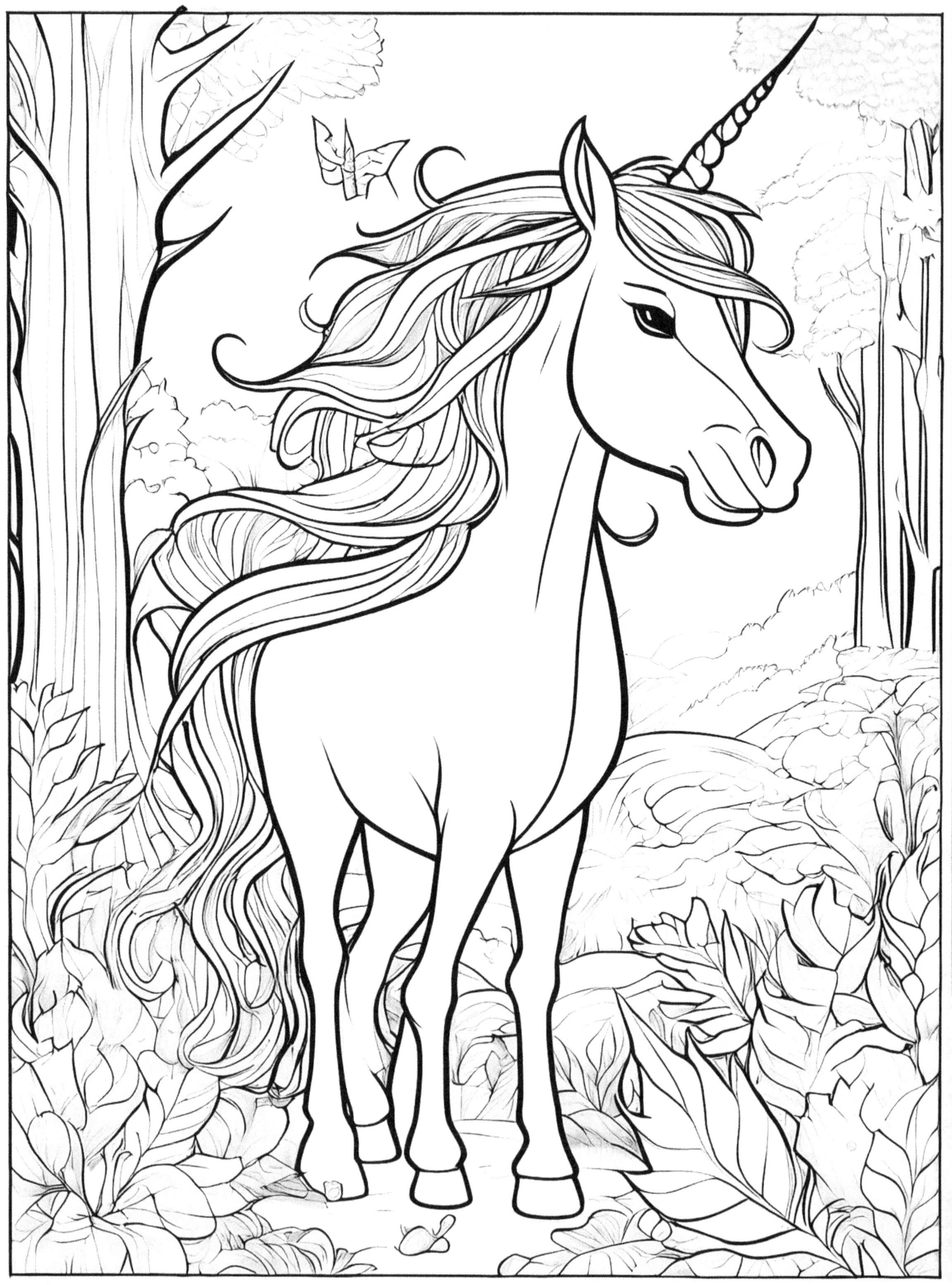

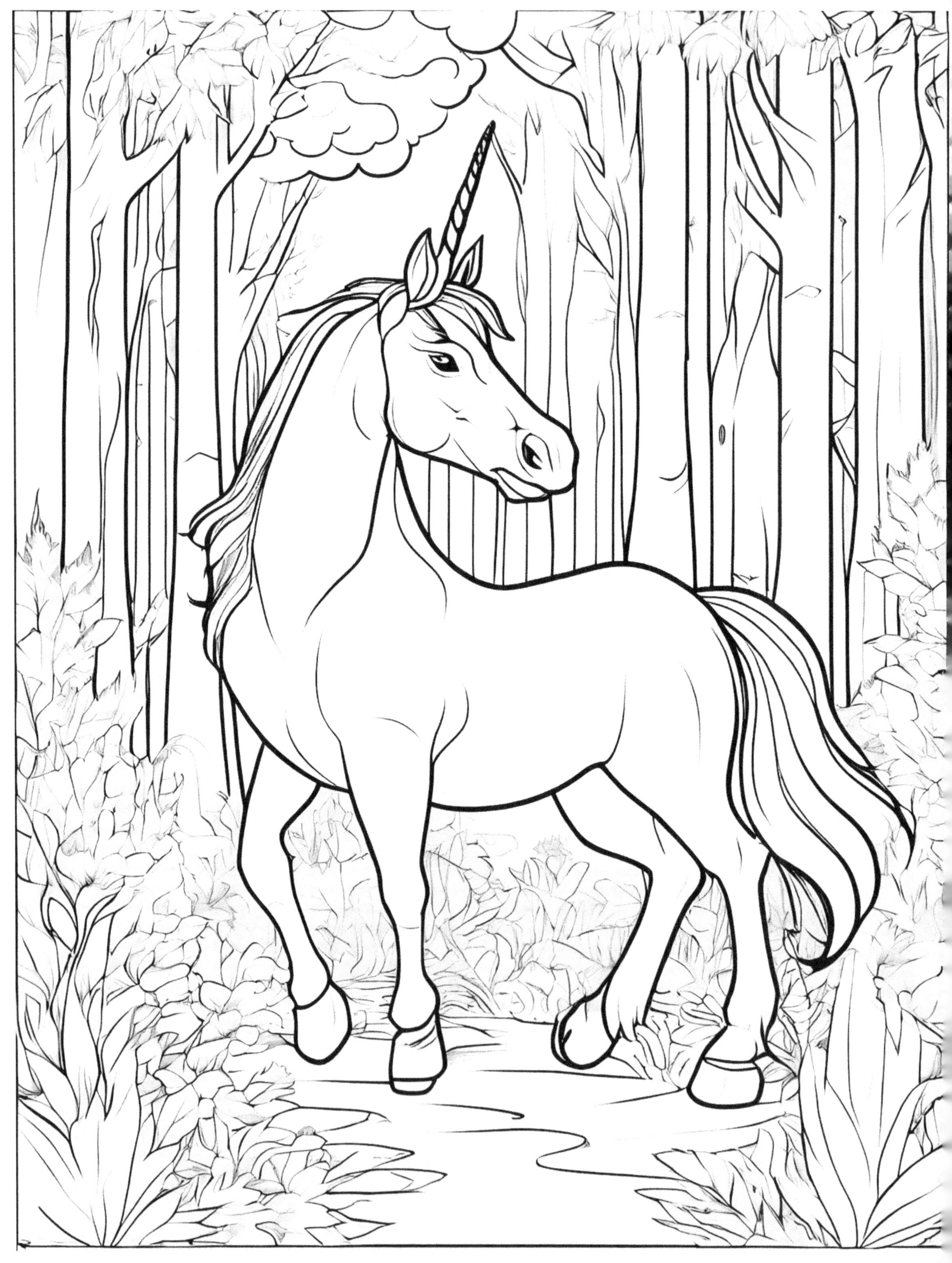

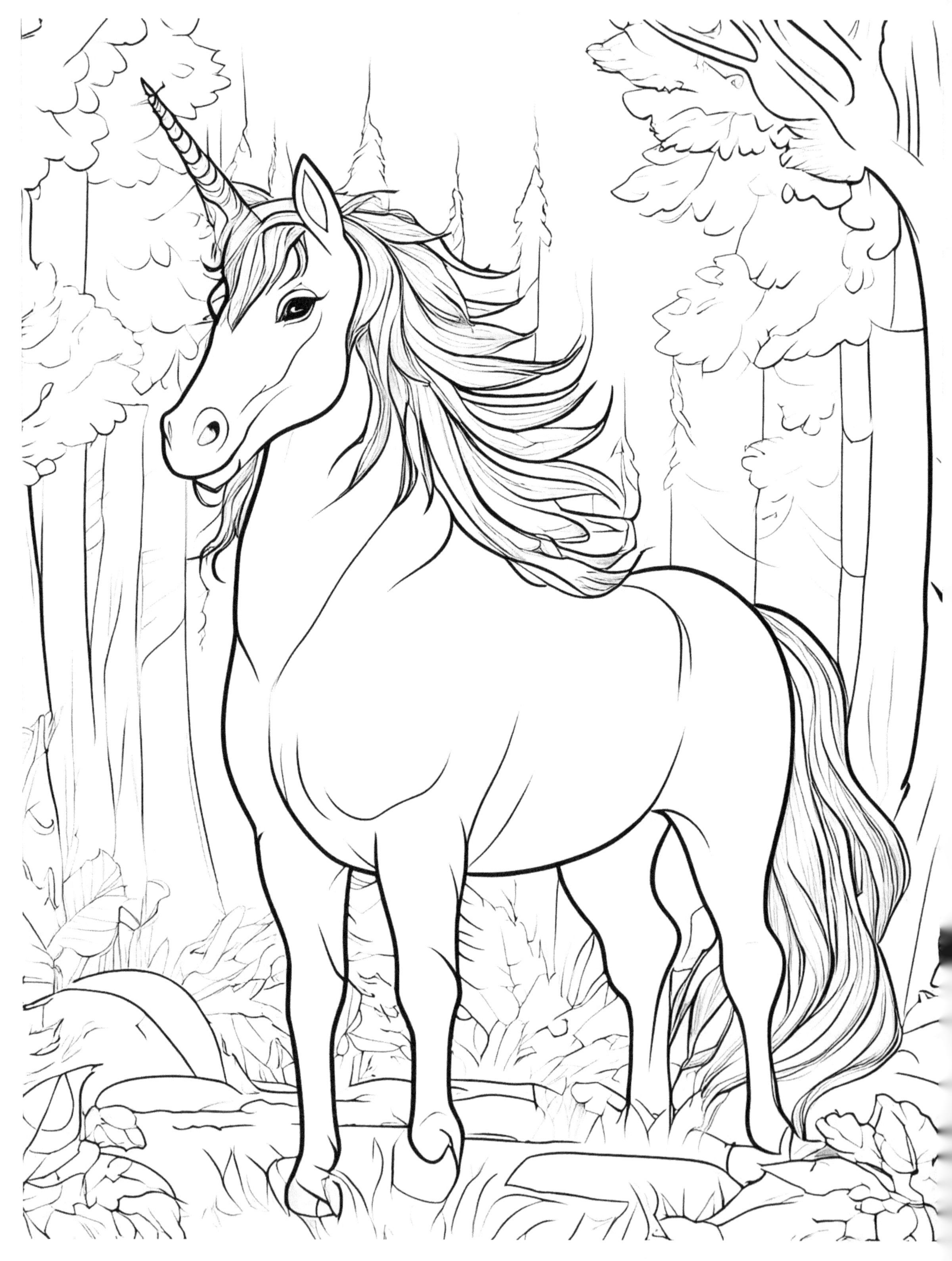

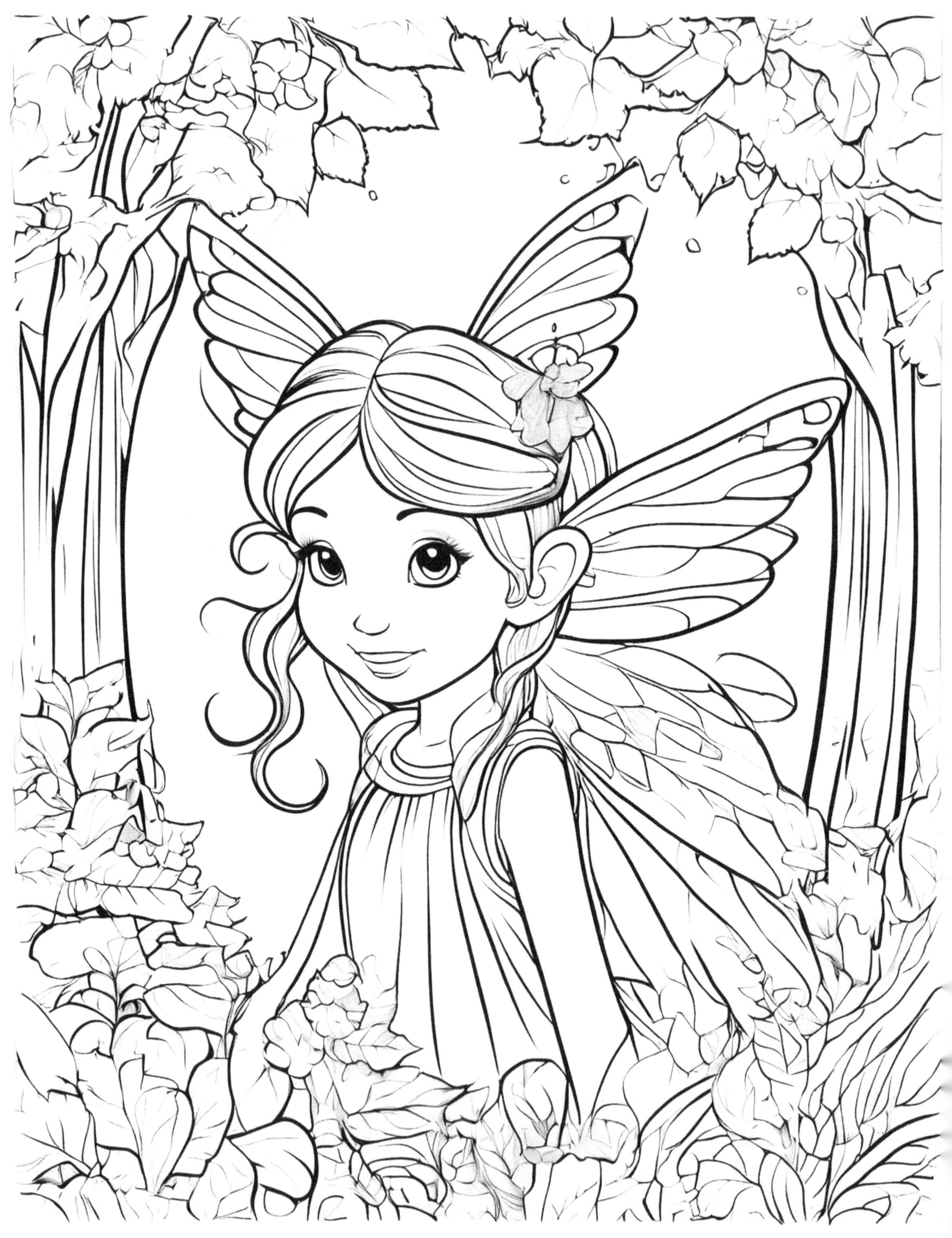

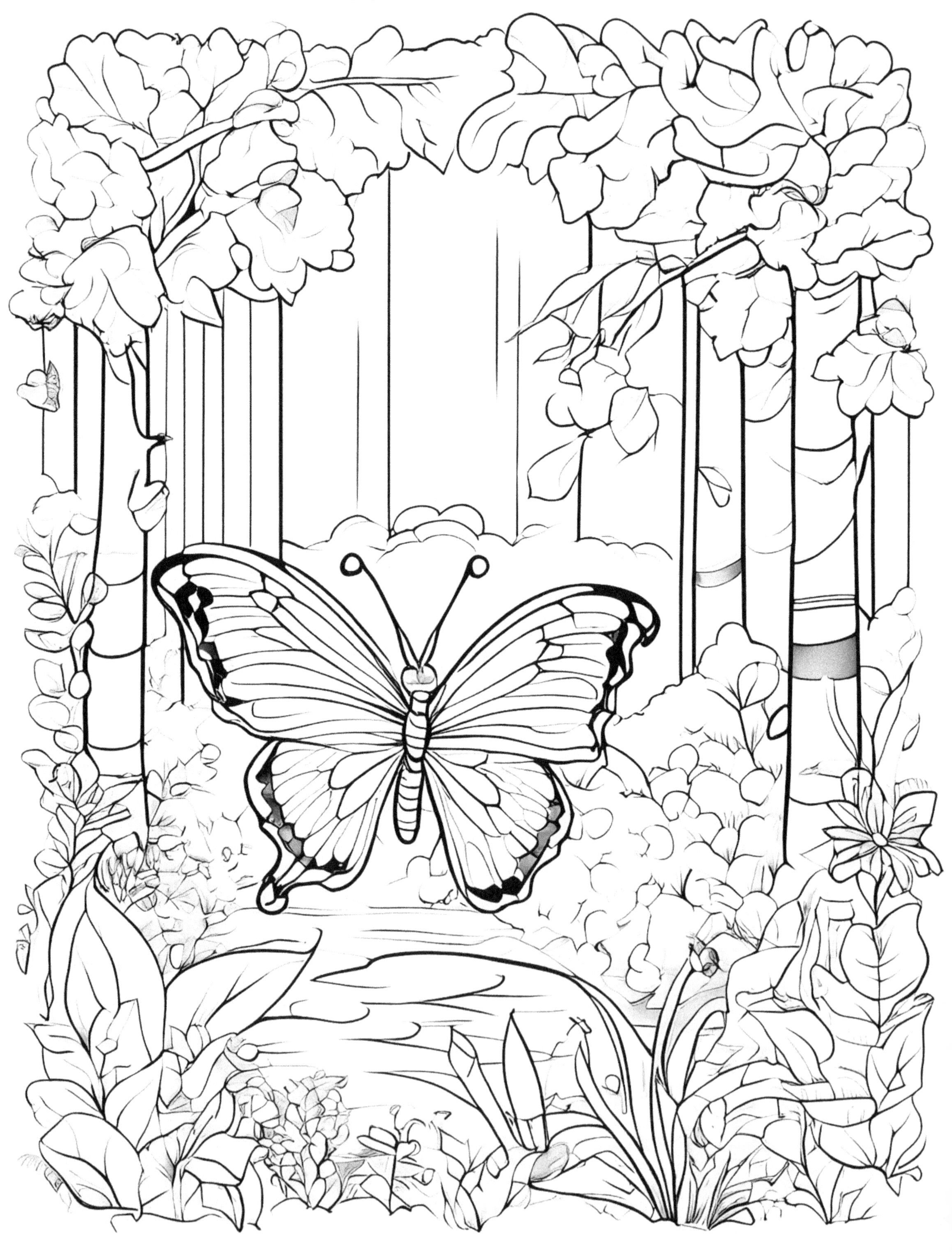

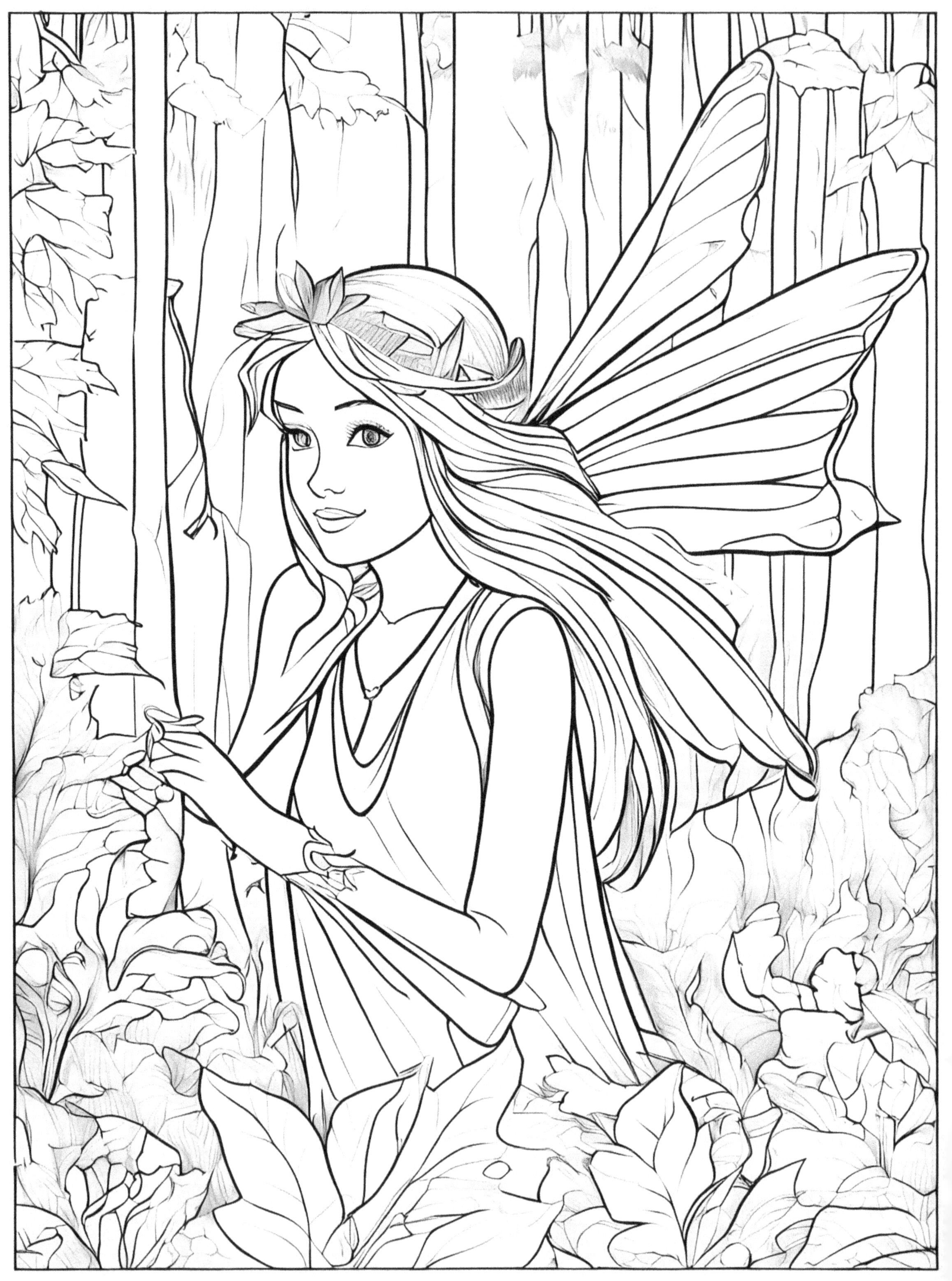

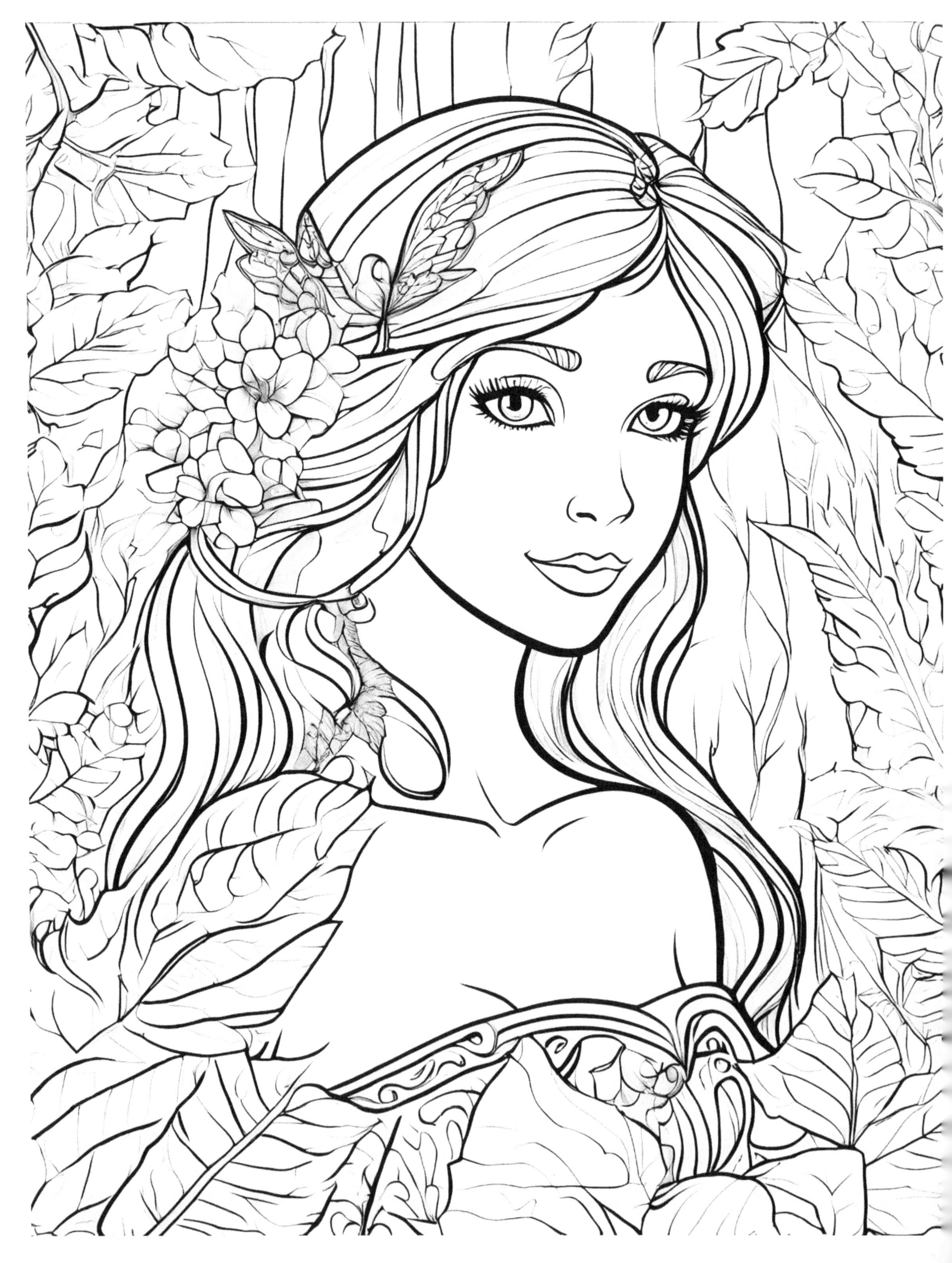

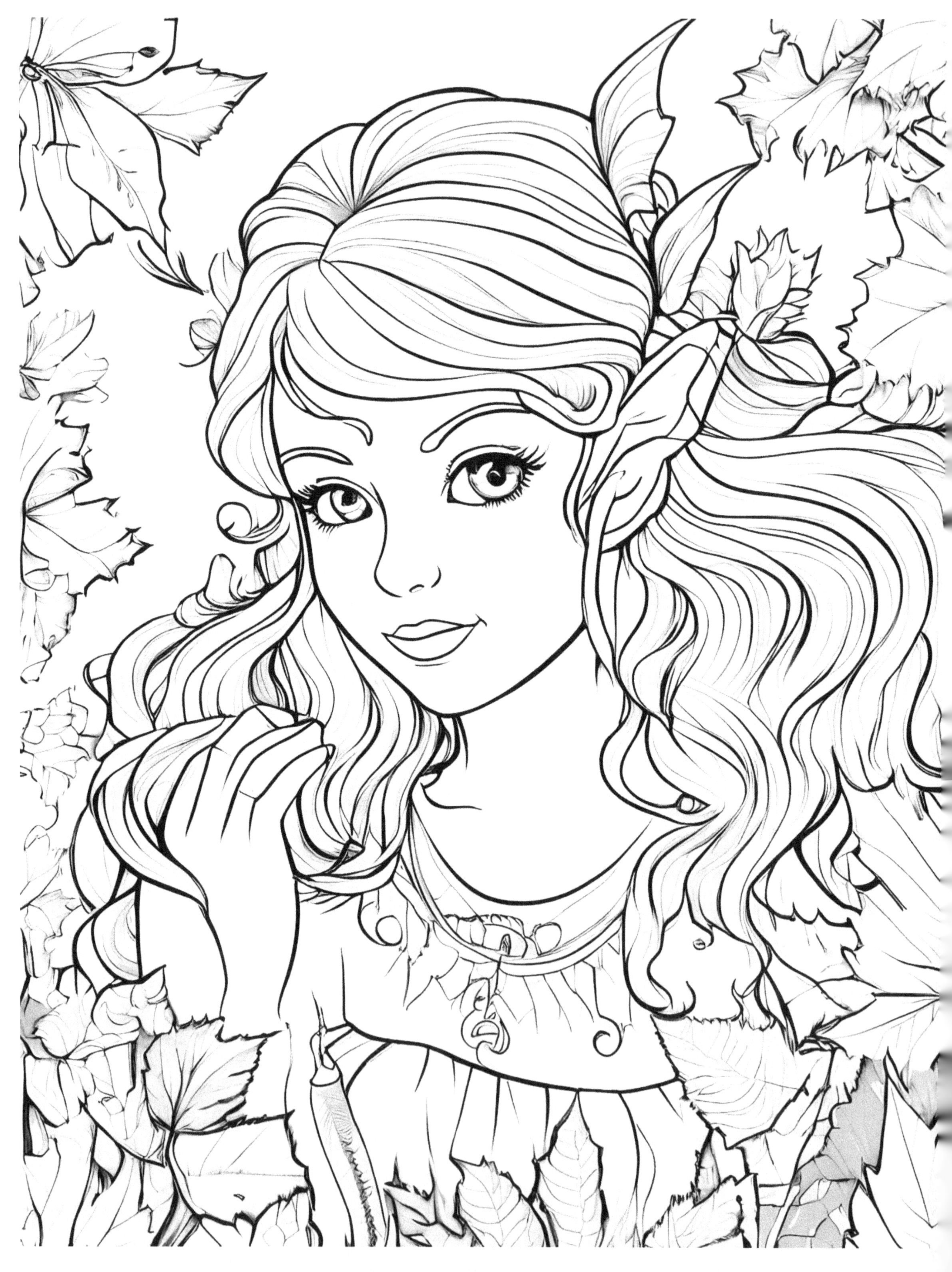

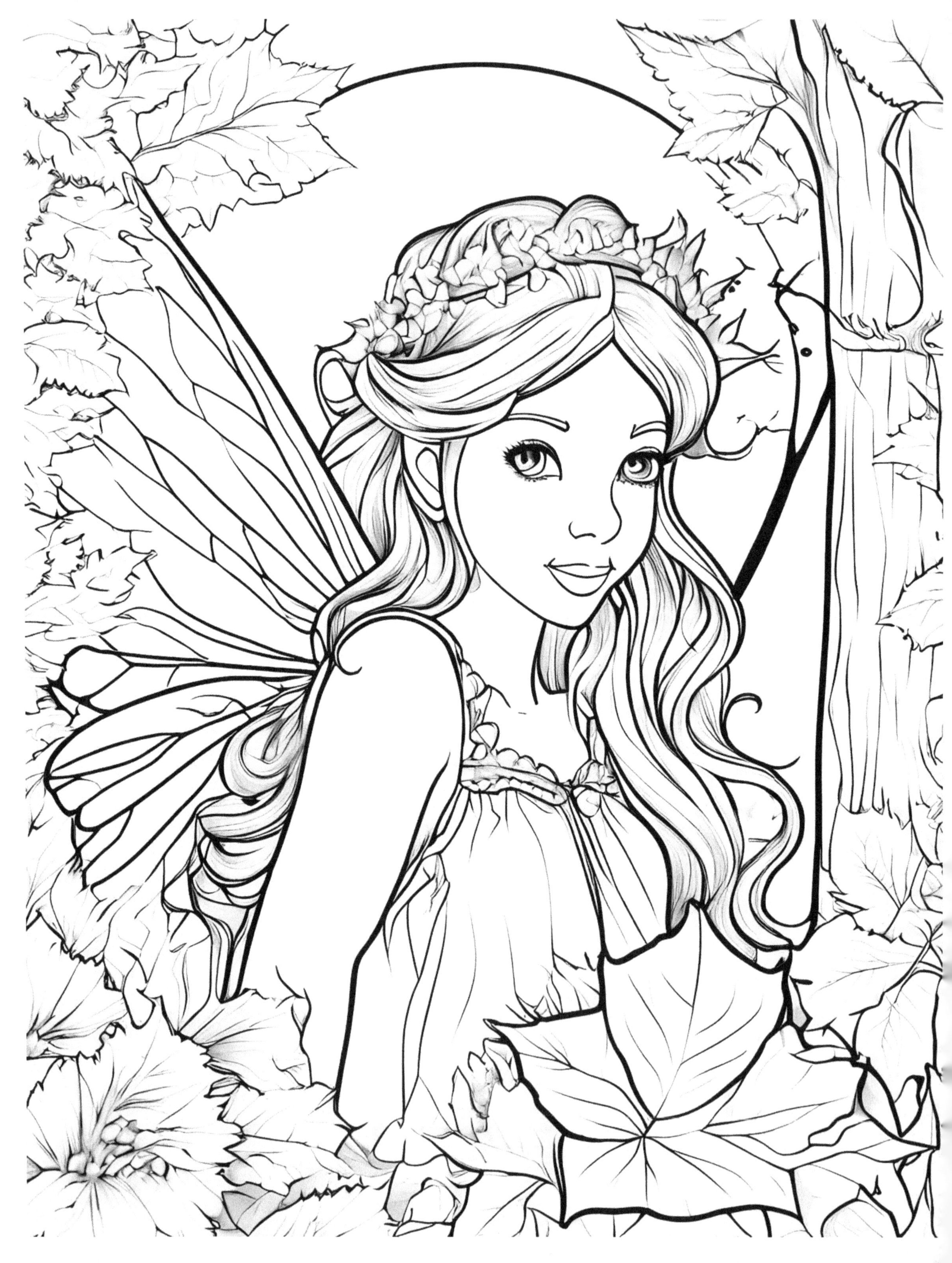

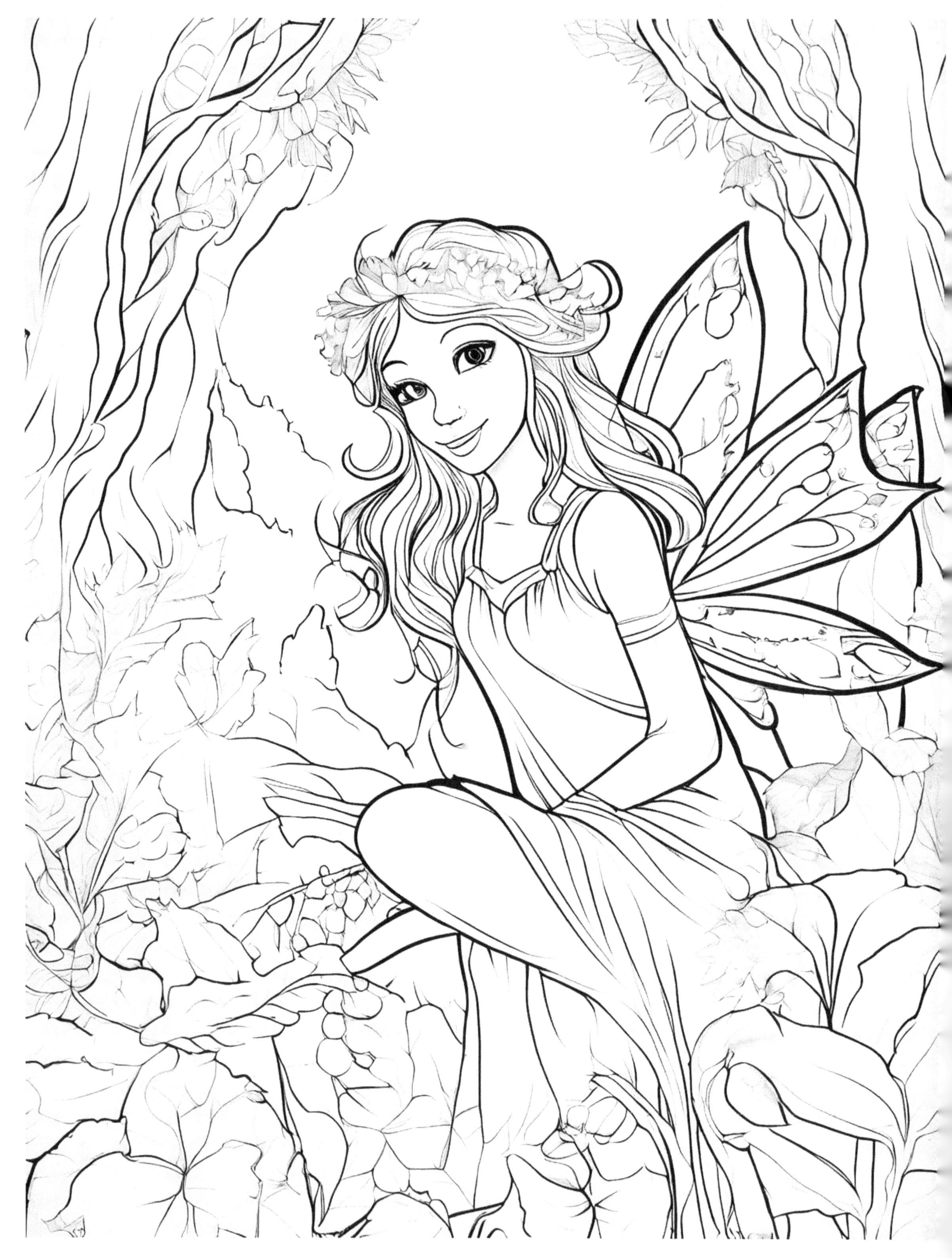

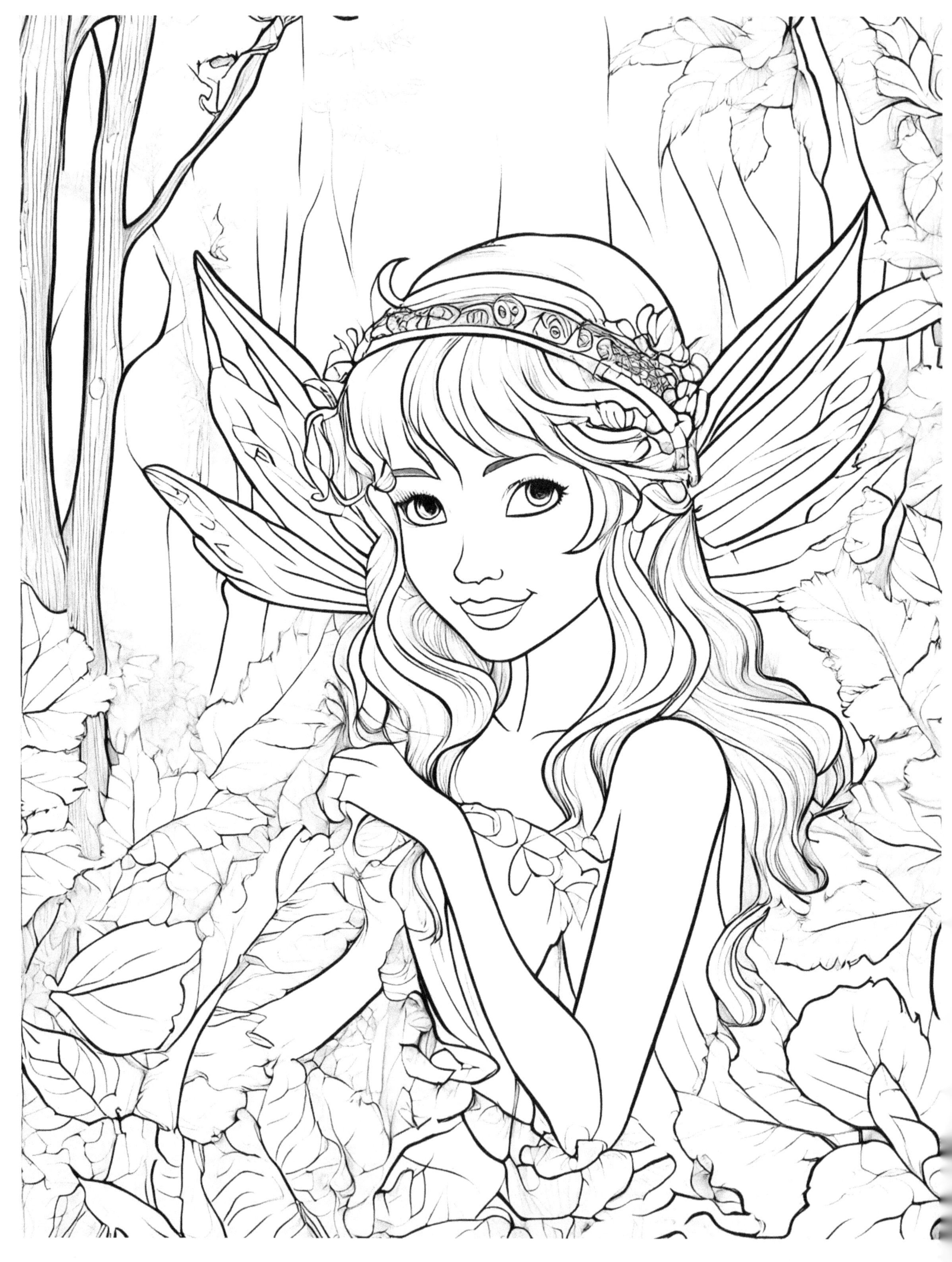

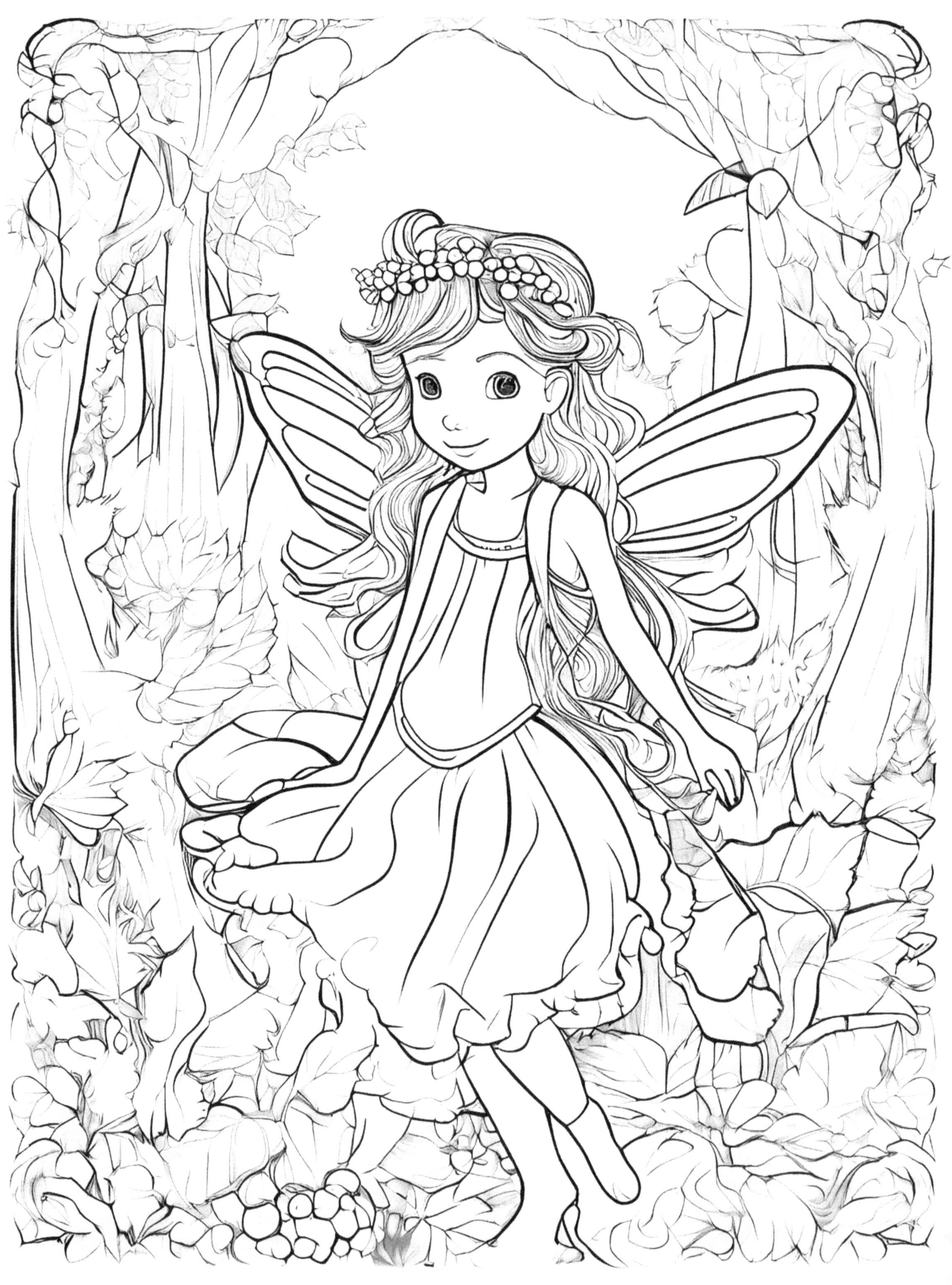

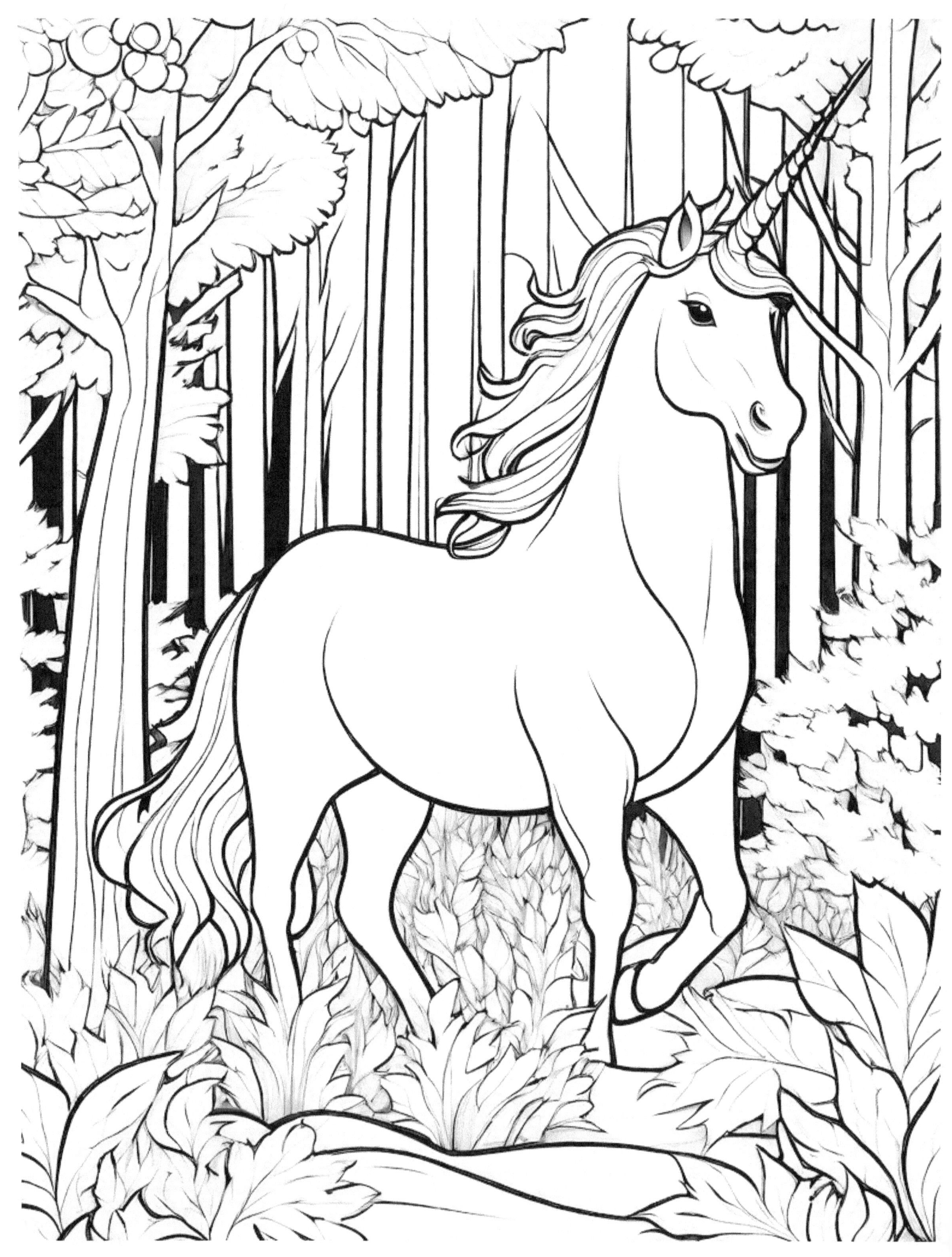